"There is a tremendous benefit to [...] shows so well in *Songs of the Son*, [...] them in light of the life, death, a[nd ... of Jesus Christ]. Focusing on the psalms used by the author of Hebrews, Stevens instructs us in how to read the Psalms in light of the whole Scripture and the whole gospel."

    Tim Challies, author, *Seasons of Sorrow*

"This delightful book is beautifully written, rooted in careful scholarship, and pastorally sensitive. One does not have to agree with every detail of the author's readings to appreciate their aid in embracing the Psalms in deeply Christian ways. The way Stevens moves to and fro between the Psalms and the letter to the Hebrews is a profoundly refreshing model of how to read Psalms in the light of the whole Bible."

    Christopher Ash, Writer in Residence, Tyndale House, Cambridge; author, *The Psalms: A Christ-Centered Commentary*

"Some books promise much more than they actually deliver; Daniel Stevens has done the opposite and given us an elegant book that is more like a multivolume feast. Delightfully conceived and skillfully executed, Stevens's book becomes our guide to reading not just the psalms quoted in Hebrews, and not just Hebrews, but the whole Psalter and even the whole Bible. He achieves this by combining profoundly rich theology, beautiful Christology, and the simple accessibility of the gifted teacher who knows how to edify and nourish with the written word. This is a superb work for all who want to understand the Scriptures more clearly and know Christ more deeply."

    David Gibson, Minister, Trinity Church, Aberdeen; author, *The Lord of Psalm 23: Jesus Our Shepherd, Companion, and Host*

"We are to be instructed by the New Testament in how to read the Old Testament. Stevens shows us that Hebrews views the Psalms as the songs of the eternally begotten Son, Jesus Christ. He is not only the subject of the Psalms but often the speaker of the Psalms. Read this book and be equipped to read the whole Bible as a compass pointing to Christ."

    Patrick Schreiner, Associate Professor of New Testament and Biblical Theology, Midwestern Baptist Theological Seminary; author, *The Mission of the Triune God* and *The Kingdom of God and the Glory of the Cross*

"An engaging and gifted writer, Daniel Stevens will help even the most experienced interpreters to read the book of Hebrews and the Psalms more faithfully and, thus, treasure Christ more deeply."

    Robert Plummer, Collin and Evelyn Aikman Professor of Biblical Studies and Chairman, New Testament Department, The Southern Baptist Theological Seminary

"If all this book did was demystify Hebrews for you, it would be worth reading. If all it did was help you read the Psalms better, it would be worth reading. If all it did was magnify Jesus, it would be worth reading. But somehow it manages to do all three in a way that is simultaneously unassuming, warm, and edifying. Read it and discover for yourself the manifold beauty of God's beloved Son through two of the Bible's most beloved books."

Peter Gurry, Associate Professor and Codirector, Text & Canon Institute, Phoenix Seminary

Songs of the Son

Songs of the Son

Reading the Psalms with the Author of Hebrews

Daniel Stevens

Foreword by Thomas R. Schreiner

WHEATON, ILLINOIS

Songs of the Son: Reading the Psalms with the Author of Hebrews
© 2025 by Daniel Stevens
Published by Crossway
        1300 Crescent Street
        Wheaton, Illinois 60187
All rights reserved. No part of this publication may be reproduced, stored in a retrieval system, or transmitted in any form by any means, electronic, mechanical, photocopy, recording, or otherwise, without the prior permission of the publisher, except as provided for by USA copyright law. Crossway® is a registered trademark in the United States of America.
Cover design and illustration: Jordan Singer
First printing 2025
Printed in the United States of America
Unless otherwise indicated, Scripture quotations are from the ESV® Bible (The Holy Bible, English Standard Version®), © 2001 by Crossway, a publishing ministry of Good News Publishers. Used by permission. All rights reserved. The ESV text may not be quoted in any publication made available to the public by a Creative Commons license. The ESV may not be translated in whole or in part into any other language.
All emphases in Scripture quotations have been added by the author.
Trade paperback ISBN: 978-1-4335-9213-3
ePub ISBN: 978-1-4335-9215-7
PDF ISBN: 978-1-4335-9214-0

Library of Congress Cataloging-in-Publication Data
Names: Stevens, Daniel, 1990- author.
Title: Songs of the son : reading the Psalms with the author of Hebrews / Daniel Stevens ; foreword by Thomas R. Schreiner.
Description: Wheaton, Illinois : Crossway, 2025. | Includes bibliographical references and index.
Identifiers: LCCN 2024005057 (print) | LCCN 2024005058 (ebook) | ISBN 9781433592133 (trade paperback) | ISBN 9781433592140 (pdf) | ISBN 9781433592157 (epub)
Subjects: LCSH: Bible. Psalms—Commentaries. | Bible. Hebrews—Criticism, interpretation, etc.
Classification: LCC BS1430.3 .S76 2025 (print) | LCC BS1430.3 (ebook) | DDC 227/.8706—dc23/eng/20240708
LC record available at https://lccn.loc.gov/2024005057
LC ebook record available at https://lccn.loc.gov/2024005058

Crossway is a publishing ministry of Good News Publishers.
VP   34   33   32   31   30   29   28   27   26   25
15   14   13   12   11   10   9   8   7   6   5   4   3   2   1

To Hannah,
whose sacrificial care for our family allowed this book to be written

Contents

Foreword by Thomas R. Schreiner   xi

Introduction   1

1   Psalm 2   9
2   Psalm 8   21
3   Psalm 22   35
4   Psalm 40   51
5   Psalm 45   65
6   Psalm 95   79
7   Psalm 102   95
8   Psalm 110   111
9   Psalm 118   131

Conclusion   147

Appendix: Why Not Psalm 104?   153
Further Reading   155
General Index   157
Scripture Index   161

Foreword

CHRISTIANS HAVE WRESTLED WITH how to interpret the Old Testament Scriptures from the outset of church history, and with the dawn of historical critical scholarship, Christological readings were frowned upon as impositions on the meaning of Old Testament texts in their original contexts. But in recent decades, Christological readings of the Old Testament are making a comeback, and the retrieval can't be chalked up to simplistic or alien readings of the Old Testament witness. Many scholars now advance the thesis that the New Testament authors read the Old Testament as it should be read.

In my judgment every Old Testament text should first be read in its original context, what Tremper Longman calls a first reading. Still, the first reading doesn't signal the end of the enterprise since we are also to follow the example of Jesus and the apostles and read the Old Testament canonically, or we could say Christologically. Both Testaments form the matrix for interpreting and understanding the biblical witness. If we ignore the Old Testament historical context, our interpretations will be ethereal and perhaps even gnostic, lacking the thickness and concreteness of the original setting. At the same time, the Old Testament points forward and has a prophetic character (Rom. 16:26). The New Testament casts light on obscure or difficult Old Testament texts (it is a mystery revealed!), but the Old Testament also runs from prophecy to fulfillment so that all God's promises are yes and amen in Jesus (2 Cor. 1:20).

This brings me to this delightful and instructive book by Daniel Stevens in which he considers texts from the Psalms that appear in Hebrews. He limits the scope to instances where Hebrews sees a reference to Jesus in the Psalms. I was struck by the creativity of the project, yet it isn't merely creative but also illuminating and fascinating. Stevens considers the Old Testament context of each psalm and then reflects on how the psalm is used in Hebrews. The book is accessible and pastoral, sure to edify and strengthen the faith of readers. Readers are also treated to a profound and deep reading of both Hebrews and the particular text from the psalms appropriated by the author. Stevens demonstrates that the author of Hebrews didn't distort or misinterpret the psalms. The way the author of Hebrews interprets these psalms functions as a pattern and paradigm for our reading of Psalms and the entire Old Testament today. It is rare when a book is both creative and faithful, but both can be said of this work by Daniel Stevens.

Thomas R. Schreiner
JAMES BUCHANAN HARRISON PROFESSOR
OF NEW TESTAMENT INTERPRETATION
ASSOCIATE DEAN OF THE SCHOOL OF THEOLOGY
THE SOUTHERN BAPTIST THEOLOGICAL SEMINARY

Introduction

Let us keep him before our eyes as we listen to the psalm. Pay close attention, beloved, for it is the discipline and teaching of our school, and it will empower you to understand not this psalm only but many others.

AUGUSTINE, EXPOSITION 2 OF PSALM 90[1]

I HAVE OFTEN HAD an uneasy relationship with the Old Testament. I have loved it for its wild poetry and intricate narrative. I have striven to see it as it came to Israel and was received in unfolding splendor. And so, throughout much of my Christian life thus far, while I have been able to see the Old Testament as God's word to Israel and as a densely woven set of storylines and movements that find resolution in the New, I have had difficulty moving back from the New Testament to the Old.

When I saw the New Testament's use of Old Testament passages, I became confused. I held the apostles' interpretations at arm's length because it seemed that they were seeing what was not there. I knew the apostles could not be wrong in their inspired

---

[1] Augustine, *Expositions of the Psalms*, vol. 4 (Ps 73–98), trans. Maria Boulding, ed. John E. Rotelle (New York: New City Press, 2002), 330.

writing, so for years I attributed this seemingly creative strand of interpretation to their role as prophets. God let them see what we otherwise could not. We should not go one letter beyond what they said and saw anew. How could we?

I had thought my problem was strictly with the New Testament and its ways of reading. In truth, I did not yet understand the Old Testament for what it really is. I had not yet learned to read the books of the old covenant as Christian Scripture. This book is about one particular implication of what that means. It is not just that the Old Testament historically led to the New Testament as a kind of prelude but rather that the one God who speaks in both Testaments intends them to belong forever to the church as a single body of Scripture. That is, while it is important—necessary even—to read the Old Testament as that which went before the coming of Christ and his gospel in all its historical rootedness as God interacted with Israel, it is just as necessary to read it alongside the New Testament as God's present word to the church. God spoke in the Old Testament, yes, and in that historical speech God still speaks. That is fundamentally what the New Testament authors knew; and that is the key to seeing, as they did, the many-splendored revelation of God in Christ that reverberates through every page of Scripture, Old and New.

This book is an attempt to reflect on how one book of the New Testament, Hebrews, guides us to better understand one book of the Old Testament, Psalms. My hope is that through reading these texts together, we may grow in our understanding and love for the God who spoke many times and in many ways through the prophets and who now, through all of his word, speaks to us in his Son.

INTRODUCTION

Why Psalms?

The Psalms have always been at the heart of Christian worship. Believers sing, pray, and meditate on the words of the Psalms week in and week out, and they have done so since the foundation of the church. This frequent devotion, however, is often only partially formed. We go to the Psalms looking to find ourselves, to put words to the emotions we already feel or hope to feel. We go to the Psalms as a voice for our heart, as a counselor, as a comfort. None of this is wrong—it is part of why God gave us the Psalms—but it is incomplete.

If we look to the way the New Testament uses the Psalms, we will discover that in addition to an emotional outpouring to God, the New Testament authors find a rich theology of God in the Psalter. The Psalms, in the New Testament's reading, are the songs of the Son. The Father speaks to the Son, and the Son speaks in return.[2] It is not just that some psalms predict things about Jesus; it is that in many of the psalms, we hear the voice of Jesus speaking and the Father speaking to him. The Son speaks in his preincarnate glory. He speaks in his earthly life and suffering. He even speaks in the role of his people, taking their sin and their suffering onto himself.

Paul, the unknown author of Hebrews and Jesus himself all go to the Psalms to find Jesus, the Son of God, speaking and being spoken to. In earlier eras, the church has been more conscious of this, singing the Psalms regularly and finding the words of Jesus in their mouths even as they saw Jesus singing their own thoughts, emotions, and confessions through the Psalter. More than any

---

2 While this type of observation is common in the older theological tradition, in modern scholarship on Hebrews it has been most clearly argued in Madison Pierce, *Divine Discourse in the Epistle to the Hebrews: The Recontextualization of Spoken Quotations of Scripture* (Cambridge: Cambridge University Press, 2020).

other book of the Old Testament, the Psalms presents us with the unity between Christ and his people as the psalmists quickly shift between speaking of the Son in his glory, in his humility, and in his representation of his people. Theophylact, a medieval Greek bishop whose New Testament commentaries proved influential in both the Western and Eastern churches, would generalize from specific quotations and claim that Paul read entire psalms as being about Jesus. This was likely uncontroversial. This is not to say that an interpretation is right because it is old or was widely accepted; but in this case, those Scripture-saturated Christians were more sensitive to the Bible's own way of reading itself. The Psalms are, in their fullness, the songs of the Son, the hymnbook of the greater David.

This is plain throughout the New Testament, but it is particularly poignant in the epistle to the Hebrews.

Why Hebrews?

In the book of Hebrews, we are presented with the God who speaks. He speaks to us in his word and in his Son. But this is not all we see. The Father speaks to the Son, and the Son speaks back. The author finds throughout Scripture, but particularly in the Psalms, this call and response within the Trinity. A divine conversation plays out before our eyes as the world is made, as salvation is accomplished, and as all things are made new in the Son of God. Our God is a speaking God, and before he ever spoke to us, God has always been the one who speaks within the Trinity. As this speaking God turns to that which is not himself, all creation bursts into being and is sustained by that same word. Within history, God speaks again and again, until at last that Son comes in whom God communicates perfectly and finally. By grace, Hebrews gives us glimpses of this divine conversation. To do so, the author turns to the language of the Psalms.

INTRODUCTION

While any book of the New Testament could be used to help us understand God's revelation in the Old, few books offer as extended, deep, and explicit an interaction with the Old Testament as does the epistle to the Hebrews. In particular, in this one letter, we are shown time and again how the Psalms form our understanding of Jesus: his nature, his work, and his relationships. Through paying close attention to how Hebrews reasons with the Psalms, we will see Jesus more clearly and learn to read the Psalms the apostles' way, as the songs of the Son.

More than any other inspired writer, the author of Hebrews develops his argument by reasoning with the Scriptures of Israel and particularly with the Psalms. Far more than simply quoting the Psalms as illustrations or proof texts, the author of Hebrews composes his entire letter as a series of arguments from the Psalms and other Old Testament texts in light of Jesus's life, death, resurrection, ascension, ongoing work, and coming return.

Nowhere else do we have such a dense and sustained interaction with one book of Scripture by another. While the author weaves together texts from all of the Old Testament canon, deftly synthesizing the Law, the Prophets, and the Writings as he demonstrates the superiority of Christ, it is to the Psalms that he returns again and again. At crucial points in his argument as he explains or applies or clarifies, the author of Hebrews reaches consistently for the Psalms. Since this is the case, it will be particularly helpful for us to explore how the author reads the Psalms.

Reading Again

There are books that demand a second reading. All the great books do. Masters of the literary craft can structure their stories in such a way that the beginning gains new significance—gains its true significance—only in light of the end. A second reading of an Agatha Christie mystery is an entirely different experience than the first. In the first reading, you are the amateur detective. You are tasked with identifying which clues are, and are not, significant. On a second reading, however, it is as if you are reading with Christie herself. She shows you how to compose a good tale, how to build suspense, how to misdirect an investigation, how to hide a clue in plain sight.

The books of the Bible also demand rereading. That we know Jesus will be crucified and raised does not diminish the power of the Gospel narratives, but rather it fills every event and saying with more meaning. When in Mark's Gospel the first human to recognize Jesus as the Son of God is the centurion at Jesus's death, we are led to a greater understanding of Mark 1:1: "The beginning of the gospel of Jesus Christ, the Son of God." We see only then that Jesus's nature and role as God's Son is understood not chiefly in his teaching or his miracles but in his death. The Son of God is the one who died for us. We cannot understand him otherwise.

This pattern is true not only for particular biblical books but also for the Bible as a whole. The garden gains new meaning from Revelation's garden city. We understand that God spoke heaven and earth into being more when we know that "in the beginning was the Word" (John 1:1).

As we read the Psalms together, we will self-consciously read them again. Of course, I do not imagine that you have never read the Psalms before. You may read them often, even daily. In this book, we will read them again. In each chapter, we will look twice at every psalm that Hebrews cites. We will read and then read again. In our first reading, I will point out the basic themes of each psalm: what it says about God, God's people, and God's world. Then, after consulting with the author to the Hebrews, we will look back at the psalm with fresh eyes to see how the whole psalm speaks of, to, and for the Son.

Reading With

You never read the Bible alone. For good or ill, every sermon you hear, every Christian book you read, every commentary you study is somewhere in the background when you engage the Scriptures. So too is the mix of TV shows, podcasts, and internet posts that shapes how you see the world around you. The question is never whether we read with interpretive lenses but whether the lenses we use are better or worse, true or false. Something is always teaching us how to read Scripture. The faithful interpreters of the past and present are wonderful guides. Talk show hosts looking for your anger and your dollars are less so. Best of all is to be taught how to read Scripture by Scripture itself.

The Scriptures are a world unto themselves, with rich layers of meaning formed by the resonances between one text and another. Often this is implicit. Echoes and allusions are formed as one text calls to another. Sometimes, however, one biblical passage looks directly to another. The Psalms show us how to read Exodus. So do Isaiah and Matthew. And when one part of Scripture draws again and again from the well of another, we do well to pay attention. When we see that Hebrews continually argues from the Psalms, we should not only pause and consider how those quotations work—that is, how they function within the argument of Hebrews—but also linger and investigate how Hebrews reads that earlier revelation. The author of Hebrews has much to tell us about his own argument, about the superiority of Jesus. In the way that he argues, he also reveals much about his Scriptures: what they are and how they are to be read. As we strive to see what the author of Hebrews saw in the short selections of psalms that he references, we will learn how those psalms, how the whole Psalter, can be read. We must not miss these lessons. Only at these times can we see infallible interpretation. Only in these moments of inspired exegesis can we precisely know how God would have us read his words. Only by reading with Scripture can we be perfectly taught how to read Scripture.

It is my conviction that if we read the Psalms with the author of Hebrews, we will learn to read the Psalms for what they truly are. Their meanings will unfold as we see precisely how they witness to Christ: not only as predictions to be fulfilled but also as testimony to the very voice of God—the Father, the Son, and the Spirit. In the voice of the psalmists, the Son reveals his nature, his mission, and his relationships with his Father and his people.

If this book serves its purpose, you will not just know more about what Hebrews argues or about the handful of psalms that the author cites. Instead, you will have a fuller and more accurate view of how the Psalter as a whole works. When you return to the divine songbook of the church, you will not only see it as a window into the life of David or the worship of Israel but will also read and sing it for what it has always truly been, the songs of the Son.

1

Psalm 2

WHAT IS THE FIRST Scripture passage that calls Jesus "Christ" and "God's Son" and then speaks about his kingdom?

You might guess that such a passage occurs in Matthew since it is the first book of the New Testament and is quite concerned about the kingdom of heaven. Or you might suspect that this is a trick question and guess that it is found in Mark or Romans.

All these books, however, come far too late. The answer is Psalm 2.

Psalm 2 is often viewed along with Psalm 1 as part of an introduction to the entire Psalter. Psalm 1 speaks about the righteous man whose mind is occupied with God's word and who is blessed by the God in whom he delights. Psalm 2 suddenly zooms outward, revealing that the story of righteousness and of God's dealing with his own is not only personal but also global. There are kings and nations, thrones and scepters. We quickly find that the line in Psalm 1 that divides between the righteous and the wicked runs through all of human history. In Psalm 1 the division is based on how one responds to God's word, but in Psalm 2 the dividing line is grounded in how one responds to God's Son—that is, his Word.

CHAPTER 1

Psalm 2 will also serve as an introduction to this book. While we will consider the psalms in canonical order, not the order in which they appear in Hebrews, Psalm 2:7 happens to be the first passage of Scripture that Hebrews cites that speaks of Jesus. It begins the author's strategy of seeing the Scriptures as containing a conversation between the Father and the Son, and it will ease us into reading the Psalms both as words *about* Jesus and as the words *of* Jesus.

Of all the psalms cited in Hebrews, Psalm 2 is possibly the easiest to read in this way, or at least it's one of the most straightforward. God and his anointed one rule. The system of the world rebels against God. God's Son is exalted. Salvation and judgment hang in the balance and are determined by whether one submits to this Son of God. On this side of the Gospels, it is hard *not to* read Psalm 2 as about Jesus.

But we are getting ahead of ourselves. We will read Psalm 2 and then read it again with the author of Hebrews as our guide.

Reading Psalm 2

Psalm 2 is a song of contrasting speech. The wicked nations gather together and speak in conspiracy against God and his anointed (2:1–3). God speaks to the Son (2:4–6), and the Son declares the Father's words (2:7–9). Then at last the narrator (still the Son?) speaks to the wicked rulers of the first several verses, proclaiming the need for either joyful repentance or fearsome destruction (2:10–12). Each three-verse stanza develops this drama of global rebellion and repentance.

The Speech of the Wicked (Ps. 2:1–3)

> Why do the nations rage
>   and the peoples plot in vain?

> The kings of the earth set themselves,
>> and the rulers take counsel together,
>> against the LORD and against his Anointed, saying,
> "Let us burst their bonds apart
>> and cast away their cords from us." (Ps. 2:1–3)

The psalmist sets the stage by raising a rhetorical question: "Why do the nations rage?" (2:1). This does not mean that they are particularly angry but rather that they are acting in a way that is disturbed, restless, and agitated. The nations are bothered that the world is ruled by God, not them.

This is, of course, a global version of what is true in every human heart. To be a sinner is to want to rule your life instead of to submit to God's rules. To be a sinner who happens to be a king is to want to rule the world instead of to submit to God's rule. The psalm imagines the nations gathered at a great summit, conspiring together to overthrow the Lord.

The psalmist, however, adds one wrinkle to this global frenzy. They scheme not only against the Lord but also "against his Anointed" (2:2). The capital letter in the ESV is the translators' clue that this should be read as a title. This is not just any anointed figure, no mere priest or prophet. It is *the* Anointed of the Lord. Of course, the Hebrew word here is *mashiach*, "Messiah." Or if you were reading along in your Greek translation like the author of Hebrews was, the title would stand out to you even more clearly: they are set against the Lord and against his *christos*, his "Christ."

In the Psalms, the use of "anointed" language, "Christ" language, is distinctly Davidic. In Psalm 18:50 "his anointed" is David and his offspring. In Psalm 20:6 it is David. In Psalm 89:20 it is David again, though from the perspective of many generations later. In Psalm 2, however, we have David-like descriptions—the anointed of the Lord who sits on Zion—but this Anointed is also greater than David. When did the nations of the world conspire against King David? Can we really say that the fate of nations, salvation and judgment, all hang on how one acts towards David, the son of Jesse?

This sets up the tension that Hebrews will resolve, and it provides a key for when and how Hebrews reads Psalms Christologically: Does the text of the psalm itself create a tension that the psalm, or even the whole Old Testament, cannot resolve? If so, it may be resolved in the person and life of Jesus. Who is the Anointed of the Lord against whom all wicked nations rage? If it is not David, there is a son of David to whom we can look.

The Speech of the Father and Son (Ps. 2:4–9)

> He who sits in the heavens laughs;
>   the Lord holds them in derision.
> Then he will speak to them in his wrath,
>   and terrify them in his fury, saying,
> "As for me, I have set my King
>   on Zion, my holy hill."
>
> I will tell of the decree:
> The LORD said to me, "You are my Son;
>   today I have begotten you.
> Ask of me, and I will make the nations your heritage,
>   and the ends of the earth your possession.
> You shall break them with a rod of iron
>   and dash them in pieces like a potter's vessel." (Ps. 2:4–9)

In the face of the gathered might of all humanity arrayed against God in rebellion, God laughs. Human pride is ultimately pitiful. Babel falls babbling (Gen. 11:1–9). Babylon the great is overturned in a day (Isa. 13:1–22). No system we construct in rebellion against God can last; all will be undone by a single word from the Lord. He laughs not because human sin on a grand scale is funny but because it is futile.

The nations speak against God, scheming to throw off his rule, but the psalmist declares that God will speak against the nations:

> Then he will speak to them in his wrath,
>   and terrify them in his fury. (Ps. 2:5)

Notice that what God says will terrify those determined to rebel against him. God's word undoes human evil. But what does God say?

> As for me, I have set my King
>   on Zion, my holy hill. (Ps. 2:6)

God's solution for human wickedness is a human king. The overthrow of every wicked kingdom, every evil system, every power that turns against God, is accomplished by the King that God establishes. Again, the psalm compels us to ask, Who could this be? What human king could possibly bring an end to all unjust human power? It cannot be David, for even when he ruled, he did not order all things as God commanded. He was unfit to build the temple. He arranged Uriah's death and took his wife for himself. But if not David, then who?

Into this tension, God's Anointed, God's King, speaks:

CHAPTER 1

> I will tell of the decree:
> The LORD said to me, "You are my Son;
>   today I have begotten you." (Ps. 2:7)

Although our picture of this Anointed one is not yet clear, it has nevertheless moved more into focus. He introduces himself not by name but by title. The Lord decreed that this Anointed one, this Christ, is also God's Son. Notice the shift in person: the Anointed himself is speaking to us ("The LORD said to me"). Before he tells us what he will do, he tells us who he is.

And this, too, is language that recalls David. When God made his covenant with David, he spoke of a future son of David: "I will be to him a father, and he shall be to me a son" (2 Sam. 7:14). In context, it means that David's heir was especially singled out by God in this way. The verse goes on to speak about what will happen when David's son who will build the temple (see 2 Sam. 7:13), Solomon, sins. The tension we saw above appears again: the "Son" of Psalm 2 is like Solomon but greater than Solomon.[1]

Significantly, the Son's speech is composed of things God said to him. If to be God's son as described in 2 Samuel 7:14 is to be David's heir, then to be God's "Son" as described in Psalm 2 is to be God's heir—that is, to receive the whole world as his inheritance (Ps. 2:8–9). We find that this King is God's solution to human wickedness writ large in two ways. Either the wicked will submit to the Son and become part of his kingdom (Ps. 2:8), or they will be destroyed by him (2:9). There are two options: salvation or

---

1 We could consider this in greater depth. It is profitable to think about Jesus as another temple-building Son of David (see John 2:19–22; 1 Cor. 3:16–17; Eph. 2:13–22), but we have other matters to deal with presently.

judgment. God hands this power over to the Son, and all will be his, either by redemption or by conquest.

The story of the psalm so far is gripping. All the powerful of the world conspire in rebellion to break the rule of God and his Anointed. God will terrify them with a word that sets forward his chosen King. This King reveals himself to be God's Son, before whom every power must either bow or be shattered. If we limit ourselves to the Psalter, or even to the whole Old Testament, we are confronted with an inescapable question: Who can this one be? Who speaks in Psalm 2? Who is God's Son, God's King, God's Christ?

The Speech of the Psalmist (Ps. 2:10–12)

> Now therefore, O kings, be wise;
>   be warned, O rulers of the earth.
> Serve the Lord with fear,
>   and rejoice with trembling.
> Kiss the Son,
>   lest he be angry, and you perish in the way,
>   for his wrath is quickly kindled.
> Blessed are all who take refuge in him. (Ps. 2:10–12)

The psalmist does not answer the question of who this Son is. Instead, he prepares his way. He sketches for us the role that this Anointed one must fill. The psalm ends with a warning to the powerful, to the rulers: bow to the Son; do not be broken. Even as the Lord laughs at the folly of human wickedness, he beckons sinners to be reconciled.

The Son is a terrifying force to evildoers. In him the power of God to rule and punish is on display. In him all wicked schemes are undone, and unrighteousness comes to ruin. And yet, the psalm does not envision a shrinking obeisance nor end with gloating derision at those who bend the knee. No, while the Son is fearsome, in his service is joy, and in his shadow is blessedness. Repentance is not shame, and the Son does not hold against anyone their need to come to him. He is fierce in his judgments; he is free in his gifts. The psalm ends with a call and a promise. The call is to repent, to kiss the Son, to submit to him, and to love him. The promise is blessedness under his care.

Reading Hebrews

For to which of the angels did God ever say,

"You are my Son,
today I have begotten you"? (Heb. 1:5a)

The author of Hebrews saw in Psalm 2:7 the perfect starting point for his description of Jesus's superiority to the angels. After declaring that God's new and final revelation has come in his Son (Heb.1:2), the author wants to demonstrate just how special this Son of God is. To do that, he states a simple fact: no angel was ever called *the* son of God. Sometimes in the Old Testament the angels are collectively called "the sons of God" in the plural (e.g., Job 1:6; 2:1; 38:7; possibly also Gen. 6:2, 4; Deut. 32:8), but never is one singled out with this title. The author reflects on this and infers that the singular Son, Jesus, is superior to the angels by virtue of his sonship. Jesus is Son in a way that the angels are not. He is the only Son, even as there are many sons of God.

The fact that the author of Hebrews uses Psalm 2:7 to establish this argument tells us that he was reading Psalm 2 as we just did above. The Christ who is God's King and Son is a greater King than David and a greater Son than Solomon. The Old Testament does not mention a person who can fit the role, but the New Testament does. Jesus is the greater King, so Jesus must be the one whom God calls Son in Psalm 2:7.

I expect that you have already reached this same conclusion. Of course Jesus is the greater David, the one greater than Solomon (Matt. 12:42; Luke 11:31). But there is an additional implication that may be less obvious. If Jesus is the Son of Psalm 2:7, then he is also the *speaker* of 2:7–9:

> I will tell of the decree:
> The LORD said to me, "You are my Son." (2:7)

Psalm 2 is not only about Jesus; it also contains his words.

This means, at the very least, that when we read the Psalms sometimes Jesus directly speaks to us—not only in the sense that he inspired them but also that the psalmist speaks in the person of Christ. This may provide an interpretive key for Psalms passages we find difficult. Christ the King whose enemies are sin and death will conquer and trample his foes. Christ the fully righteous one can plead his righteousness before God. Christ the sufferer can call down judgment. This does not separate us from the Psalms. After all, Christ's people are his body, so he can speak for us too. But it does give us a theological resource for understanding difficulties. Particularly, in Psalm 2, when the text itself confronts us with tensions it cannot answer, the speech of Jesus in the psalm resolves all issues.

Incidentally, interpreters have long argued over the meaning of "today" when God said to Jesus, "You are my Son, / today I have begotten you" (2:7). Some have seen eternity in "today," reading this as referring to the eternal relationship between the Father and the Son. The Father has never not been Father; the Son has never not been Son. This "today" is without beginning or end, always happening as it has always happened. Other interpreters have understood "today" to refer to the incarnation, when God the Son became the Davidic Son. Still others have taken "today" to be fulfilled at Jesus's resurrection or at his exaltation to the right hand of the Father, when as incarnate King he rises and reigns on the heavenly throne. The second half of Hebrews 1:5, which quotes 2 Samuel 7:14 (discussed above), may sway one's reading of this. I think that the author's quotation of Psalm 2:7 emphasizes his eternal sonship—both because of the use of "today" and the fact that this Son is heir of God—while the quotation of 2 Samuel 7:14 talks about his exalted, resurrected sonship as the reigning heir of David. This does not make much difference in how you interpret either Hebrews or Psalm 2 generally; both things are clearly true of Jesus elsewhere. But if Hebrews 1:5 says that Psalm 2:7 refers to Jesus's eternal sonship, then the mention of his reign on Zion in Psalm 2:6 is likely an oblique reference to the incarnation.

Reading Psalm 2 Again

When we read Psalm 2 again, after reading Hebrews, what new insights do we find?

First, the rage of the nations, their disordered rebellion against God, is a rebellion against Christ—not against the Lord's anointed in a general sense but specifically against Jesus. Any human system built on human power and not on obedience to God is opposed to Jesus. Thus, it will eventually oppose God's commands and word. It will also oppose Christ and his people. In the Gospels, Christ predicts persecution for his people (Matt. 5:11–12; Mark 4:17;

Luke 11:49; John 15:20), and Paul assures that all who seek to live godly lives will be persecuted (2 Tim. 3:12). Psalm 2 predicts the same. It must eventually happen because the only thing that unites the powers of this world is opposition to the Lord and to his Christ.

Second, Jesus overcomes all such rebellion, either by winning over his opponents through merciful conversion or by shepherding the nations and shattering the proud with his rod of iron. Jesus suffered. Jesus's people suffer. But Jesus does not lose. He is God's solution to all opposition, to the wickedness that runs rampant in the world. His kingdom has already been established by God, and it will encompass all the nations of the earth.

Third, Jesus speaks what the Father spoke to him. We find in Psalm 2:7–9 the pattern explicitly set out in John 12:49: "For I have not spoken on my own authority, but the Father who sent me has himself given me a commandment—what to say and what to speak." In his work within creation, the Son brings the message of the Father. He says the words his Father sent him to say. Or as Hebrews 1:2 says, "In these last days [God] has spoken to us by his Son." The Son *is* the revelation of the Father. To see the Son is to see the Father (John 14:7–9). This is what Scripture means when it calls Jesus the Word of God (John 1:1) or the radiance of God's glory (Heb. 1:3). This is especially clear in the New Testament, but it is not new. In Psalm 2, hiding in plain sight, the same pattern is revealed. God the Son's actions in revelation and redemption follow the same pattern throughout salvation history, even before the incarnation, because they reflect who the Son is.

Conclusion

In Psalm 2, Jesus is called God's Christ and God's Son. He speaks God's words and calls everyone to salvation in him. The sweep of human history is summarized: the nations rage and kings scheme; all must either submit joyfully to Christ or perish. Jesus's reign, his kingdom, is God's solution to human wickedness. All peoples are his inheritance; the Father will hand them over to him. The offer of refuge in Jesus is extended to all, but those who do not find blessing in him will be shattered by his judgment.

Discussion Questions

1. What does it look like for "the nations" to rebel against God?

2. How does the author of the epistle to the Hebrews see Jesus speaking in Psalm 2?

3. What does it mean to be a part of the Son's kingdom?

4. What does Psalm 2 tell us about Jesus?

5. What does Psalm 2 tell us about ourselves?

2

Psalm 8

EVERYTHING IS SUPPOSED to be under control.

It is easy to forget what a futuristic wonderland we live in, compared even to the recent past. We can regulate the temperature of our houses to the degree. Night doesn't compel us to go to bed; we simply turn the lights on. A common killer in past generations, bacterial infection, is now resolved by a routine trip to the pharmacy. This is good. Things are supposed to be under our control. And often it feels as though they are.

Until it becomes clear that they are not.

My son was hospitalized shortly before his second birthday for emergency surgery. One moment he was happy and playing, searching for Easter eggs with friends, and the next moment he was screaming, unable to walk or tell us what was wrong. As far as the doctors and pathologists could determine, the cause was an ear infection. Somehow it had danced around the antibiotics he had taken, migrated within his body, and hidden inside his hip, where medicine could not reach it. Even though the surgeons and staff were able to help him, my sense of control was stripped away.

This small thing that we thought had been treated, that we thought was no longer a threat, came very close to taking my son's ability to walk—or worse.

Things are not in our control. Even when we forget this, even when we feel like everything can be adjusted with the press of a button or the flip of a switch, our helplessness in the face of life is only a breath away. And when we suffer tragedy or face near misses, we know deep in our bones that this is not how it is supposed to be. There is something wrong about the way people are exposed to danger, loss, and suffering at any moment. There is something tragic about the suddenness of pain. All our modern conveniences are only a veneer of shaky control that point to a reality we cannot grasp. Things are supposed to be under our control, but they are not.

This somewhat unexpected insight is what the author to the Hebrews brings to his reading of Psalm 8. God is majestic, and he has given control of his world to humanity. Yet things are not how they should be. Although Psalm 8 and Hebrews have more to say, they do not say less than this.

Reading Psalm 8

Psalm 8 is about God. The Lord's splendor over the heavens is put on display. David begins and ends with declarations of God's majestic name in all the earth. The psalm also testifies to God's glory in all scales of creation. If you look at the heavens, the stars and the galaxies, God's majesty is displayed, and his glory is higher than they. The grand expanse of the heavens and its luminaries are but the work of his fingers, small piecework of a master craftsman. But if you look down, you also see things small and near. You find God's strength and praise in nursing babies and babbling infants.

If David had a strong enough microscope, he would discover God's majesty in the dance of electrons and the structure of molecules. There is no element of cosmic experience that does not testify to God's glory.

Yes, Psalm 8 is about God. But it is also about humanity. While the psalm begins and ends with God's majesty, the majority of its verses speak of mankind. Looking back to the Genesis account, David discusses humanity in relation to God and then in relation to his creation. As he sings of God and his works, David sets out two paradoxes that are central to the story of the Bible and to Christian experience: How can God care for us when we are so small (Ps. 8:1–4)? How are we both so small and so great over the rest of creation (8:5–9)? Or to put it another way, why does God's love come to us when we are so unworthy of it, and why does his love make us so great?

Big God and Small Humans (Ps. 8:1–4)

To the choirmaster: according to The Gittith. A Psalm of David.

> O Lord, our Lord,
> how majestic is your name in all the earth!
> You have set your glory above the heavens.
> Out of the mouth of babies and infants,
> you have established strength because of your foes,
> to still the enemy and the avenger.
>
> When I look at your heavens, the work of your fingers,
> the moon and the stars, which you have set in place,
> what is man that you are mindful of him,
> and the son of man that you care for him? (Ps. 8:1–4)

David begins with the majesty of God as Creator. The majesty—the greatness—of the name of God is evident in all the world. Even above the heavens, in the heights of the expanse and beyond, God's glory is manifest. No heavenly sphere, no angelic host can compare. All are under the greatness of the Lord. And even in the small and weak, God's greatness and power are displayed. Humanity first enters the picture in Psalm 8 in the form of "babies and infants" (8:2)—that is, humanity at its weakest and smallest. Babies cannot even lift their own heads, but in them the strength of God is seen. Infants cannot speak, yet from their mouths the Lord's praise comes. How can this be? And who are "the enemy and the avenger" (8:2) that this praise stills?

While we find in the New Testament additional ways in which this passage is fulfilled (such as when small children recognize Jesus as Lord in Matt. 21:16 and, more broadly, Jesus's teaching that the kingdom of God belongs to such little ones in Matt. 18:1–10), here the primary way in which infants declare the praise of the Lord must be parallel to how the heavens show God's glory. In God's intricate crafting of every human child, in his sustaining power that upholds those who cannot uphold themselves, in the wisdom of his plan that children should come into existence at all, God's power and glory are made known. To see a child is to see the wonderful creative power of God on display. To hold an infant is to hold a work of God no less wondrous than a star.

And the enemies? They are unlikely the enemies of the infants but rather God's enemies. To call them "avengers" likely means something more like the "vindictive," those who suppose themselves to have been wronged by God. They see the wonderful power of God in creation and despise it. They contend that the world should not be as God made it, that he does not know what he is doing. Such people are like those who would throw off God's rule in Psalm 2. These enemies are stilled by the strength of God evident in the coos of an infant. One honest look at the wonders around us, one clear glimpse at what an unimaginably splendid thing a human child really is, and any mouth speaking against God's work in creation must be stopped.

In all this, God shines as great. Even the heavens, the moon and stars in their courses, are "the work of [God's] fingers" (Ps. 8:3). The words the psalmist uses matter. To speak of the heavenly bodies as the work of God's fingers is to imagine the grandest galaxy or the largest star as a small work of his artistry. They are not great exertions for God. They are not big to him. They are details of his finesse. It is in this light, when the expanse of the heavens is shown to be no great tapestry but a small embroidery of God, that we get a sense of our own human scale. David looks up at the innumerable stars, senses the immensity of God, and exclaims,

> What is man that you are mindful of him,
> and the son of man that you care for him? (Ps. 8:4)

The wonder of it all, though, is that God does care for us. There is a modern impulse that sees the vastness of space, the near endless cold expanse between errant rocks and smoldering stars, and treats this as an argument *against* God's love for us. We think of space as empty and largely pointless, and thus it stands as a mute witness against the possibility of a loving God. How, we think, in the face of such enormous waste and confusion, could the God who made it even notice us? How could that God of endless black and countless galaxies love you?

Psalm 8 reads reality in the entirely opposite way. The expanse of the heavens is not idle; it declares God's glory. Precisely in its greatness and its mind-boggling testimony to the infinite greatness of God, it bears witness to this fact: God's love for you is bigger than this. He made the heavens as grand as they are to give us a hint of how much he cares for us. Exactly in our smallness, he is mindful of us. If you still find yourself too small in the face of all that God is and has made, know that this only makes you fit more firmly in his hands.

The universe is not a vast, silent void in which God must find us; it is the chorus that God assigned to sing to us the theme of his greatness and love. If our sense of space is bigger than David's was, if we can speak of lightyears and billions of galaxies, how much more powerfully can we speak the testimony of Psalm 8? God made all this, and he cares for us.

Small Humans over a Big Creation (Ps. 8:5–9)

> Yet you have made him a little lower than the heavenly beings
> > and crowned him with glory and honor.
> You have given him dominion over the works of your hands;
> > you have put all things under his feet,
> all sheep and oxen,
> > and also the beasts of the field,
> the birds of the heavens, and the fish of the sea,
> > whatever passes along the paths of the seas.
>
> O LORD, our Lord,
> > how majestic is your name in all the earth! (Ps. 8:5–9)

God's care for us is not vague. Psalm 8 describes his attention to us in terms of exaltation. From the beginning, God created humanity to be great, to exercise dominion over all he had made.

PSALM 8

David speaks the language of creation and looks back to the Genesis account. God made man in his image (Gen. 1:26–27)—that is, to be like God and represent him. Then he blessed humanity (Gen. 1:28) by giving us rule over creation under him (1:26, 28–30). David turns this description of God's work into a song of praise. The Lord made humanity "a little [or "for a little while"] lower than the heavenly beings" (Ps. 8:5), likely meaning angels. Though we are small, we are also "crowned . . . with glory and honor" (Ps. 8:5). We are God's vice-regents.

The mention of "all things" and, specifically, "the works of [God's] hands" (Ps. 8:6) brings our attention back to the first half of the psalm. Remember that the moon and the stars are the works of God's fingers (Ps. 8:3). Even the very heavens that showcase God's greatness and our small stature are included in the "all things" placed under mankind's dominion. God's plan for humanity has a cosmic scope. (Incidentally, this is why Paul says in Rom. 8:19–23 that all creation was subjected to futility when mankind fell, because all creation was part of the cosmic rule that we were made for and abandoned.)

Psalm 8:7–8 then lists the animals (those of land, sky, and sea) in the reverse order of their creation in Genesis 1 (animals of sea, sky, and land). This structure signals that David is explicitly commenting on the text of Genesis 1 and shows that even the elements of creation made before mankind are to be subject to humanity. All things are placed under mankind's dominion (Ps. 8:6), because God intends humanity to spread his rule over his world.

David then bursts again into praise with the same words that began the psalm:

O Lord, our Lord,
    how majestic is your name in all the earth! (Ps. 8:9)

Although these may be the same words, David now sings them in a different key. At the outset, he praises God for his creative power as displayed in all levels of creation. At the end, the emphasis is on God's majesty in placing humanity, his image bearers, over all creation with everything under their control.

Reading Hebrews

And yet, everything is not under our control. This objection, this tension between the words of Scripture and our experience (and even between one biblical passage and another), is an opportunity for the author of Hebrews to find resolution through the life of Jesus. Once again, according to Hebrews, the pattern of Jesus's incarnation, suffering, death, resurrection, and ascension is the key to understanding an interpretive tension in the Psalms.

In Hebrews 2, the author turns from his argument that Jesus is superior to the angels to the fact that Jesus helps humans, not angels. In this context, he says,

> For it was not to angels that God subjected the world to come, of which we are speaking. It has been testified somewhere,
>
>> "What is man, that you are mindful of him,
>>> or the son of man, that you care for him?
>> You made him for a little while lower than the angels;
>>> you have crowned him with glory and honor,
>>> putting everything in subjection under his feet."
>
> Now in putting everything in subjection to him, he left nothing outside his control. At present, we do not yet see everything in subjection to him. (Heb. 2:5–8)

The author reads Psalm 8 carefully. He is committed to understanding the psalm as written. The author refuses to let David be imprecise. If David says "everything" is placed in subjection to man, then it must mean everything in creation, no exceptions. And yet, this is not what we see. Since Scripture must be entirely true, the author says, we have a problem. Everything is supposed to be under our control, but it is not. We suffer. Our own bodies revolt against us. We die. We face myriad dangers: natural disaster, disease, accidents, enemies. Everything is very much *not* in subjection to us.

Not *yet*, the author says.

By now you know that in some way Jesus is the solution to this interpretive difficulty, but there is a false trail I do not want us to follow. We might be tempted to read "son of man" in Psalm 8 in light of how Jesus refers to himself with this expression in the Gospels. We might conclude that the psalm was never actually about us but about Jesus the whole time. That would resolve the tension, but it would be wrong.

Hebrews does not let us read the psalm this way. Instead the author clarifies the problem: "We do not yet see everything in subjection to him" (Heb. 2:8). In subjection to whom? To man, to the son of man, to the one discussed in Psalm 8. This is precisely the problem. God subjected everything to humanity, but we do not see everything subject to us. God's word and our world seem to be in conflict. How is Jesus the solution to this dilemma? How does Jesus's work solve the problem of humanity's position in the world? Jesus's work must enable humanity to occupy the role God intended. And this, precisely, is where Hebrews goes: "But we see him who for a little while was made lower than the angels, namely Jesus, crowned with glory and honor because of the suffering of death, so that by the grace of God he might taste death for everyone" (Heb. 2:9).

The author's argument is compact. Jesus, like mankind in Psalm 8, is crowned with glory and honor. Jesus, like mankind, was made for a little while lower than the angels. Jesus's road to glory, however, first was a descent. He descended to a humble human life and even went down through death itself. In the author's discussion of Jesus in Hebrews 2, two facts from the psalm—"You made him lower" and "You crowned him" (Ps. 8:5)—are made into a sequence: Jesus was crowned because he was lowered. How does this work? And how does this affect the way we read the psalm?

Reading Psalm 8 Again

The interpretation of Psalm 8 in Hebrews only works if we realize two important theological truths. First, Jesus's incarnation matters. As Christians who glory in the cross of Christ and his death for us, it is easy to think that the only point of Jesus's incarnation was so that he could experience a bodily death. But that is not the biblical picture. Instead, when the Son of God took on human flesh, he united himself to humanity as such. He took on human nature to heal human nature. All of it.

In Hebrews 2:14–18, the author emphasizes that Jesus needed to be like us in every way. Why? So that he could heal every part of us. Gregory of Nazianzus, a fourth century theologian, put it in this pithy way: "For what is not assumed is not healed, but what is united to God is saved."[1] That is, only if Jesus is fully human can he fully heal humanity. When Adam fell, everything about what

---

[1] Gregory of Nazianzus, "Epistle 101 to Cledonius," in *Christ: Through the Nestorian Controversy*, vol. 3 in *The Cambridge Edition of Early Christian Writings*, ed. Mark DelCogliano, trans. Bradley K. Storin (Cambridge: Cambridge University Press, 2022), 392.

it means to be human became fallen. By becoming fully human—body, soul, and spirit—Jesus laid hold of all of human nature to redeem all of it. Or to put it another way, everything Jesus does *as* a human is something Jesus does *for* humans. The whole of the incarnation is for us and for our salvation.

The second theological truth is that Jesus's incarnation, death, resurrection, and ascension reenact humanity's history. Humanity, made by God lower than the angels, was crowned by God with dominion over his creation. But we fell; we sinned. And because of our sin, we do not currently see everything in subjection to us. Because of the curse of sin that reverberates throughout the cosmos, some of the praise of Psalm 8 falls flat. We have left our position, and the world is not as it should be. But Jesus took up our ragged humanity and became lower than the angels for a little while. His descent did not stop at merely becoming a human, but he lowered himself to the point of death. Jesus took upon himself the very thing that breaks mankind's dominion over this world: the curse of sin, which is death. But Jesus did not remain dead. He rose from the grave and was lifted to God's right hand, where he sits now enthroned and crowned with glory and honor, waiting until the fullness of the kingdom.

To quote Hebrews, "We see him" (Heb. 2:9). Jesus, *as a man*, sits where humanity is supposed to sit, in dominion over all creation with all things subjected to him. And everything he does *as* a human he does *for* humans. Because we see him sitting where Psalm 8 says we should sit—in dominion over God's creation—we know that we will sit there with him. A day is coming when Psalm 8 will be true of all redeemed humanity in Christ. The exalted position God intended for mankind as his image bearers, as his representatives and regents, was not abandoned at the fall. We see it in Jesus now. We will see it in ourselves in the new creation. Hebrews talks about Jesus as a "forerunner" (Heb. 6:20) and as "founder" of our salvation and faith (2:10; 12:2). This means that he goes where we need to go, and then he brings us with him. Jesus reclaims the position God gave us that we lost through sin. And since he reclaimed it, we know that it will be ours in him.

We are not left with the tension between what Psalm 8 says about us and our own experience. Instead, because of Jesus's fulfilment of Psalm 8, we find ourselves living between God's exaltation of humanity in creation and his greater exaltation of humanity in the new creation. We see Jesus, our great forerunner, ensuring us that we will have what he now has, because he took on what we now have. What more can we do than say with the psalmist,

> O Lord, our Lord,
> how majestic is your name in all the earth! (Ps. 8:1, 9)?

Conclusion

Everything is supposed to be under control. Not just because our modern conveniences fool us into thinking so but also because God made humanity for this role. He created everything to be under the good rule of humanity, his image bearers. We are supposed to share in his rule on the earth. Yet we do not see that now. Instead, we see sin and struggle, death and destruction. But we also see Jesus, who took on our suffering, died in our place, rose again to give us his life, ascended to heaven, and sat down where we will join him. Everything is, right now, under his control. And under him, we will join in his good plan of ruling over everything God has made.

Discussion Questions

1. What did God make humanity to do?

2. How should the study of creation affect our view of God and his work?

3. How does Jesus relate to Psalm 8?

4. How does knowledge of our future help us now?

3

Psalm 22

IN MY FAMILY, we love the moon.

Sure, the sun may be showier, but there is something about the quiet and shifting beauty of the moon that captures our imagination. Especially when you have small children who are often in bed just as it grows dark, the moon becomes something like a rare delicacy, a change of pace to the constant diet of the sun's bright beams. On those rare occasions when we are driving as the sky becomes dark and the moon becomes clear, we track the path of the moon, shouting out whenever it might be visible from the back seat. Even rarer still, when the moon faintly hangs in the sky during the day, we make a point of going out to see it, being glad for its beauty even as the sun shines in all its own splendor.

All that to say, sometimes the less radiant thing has a beauty worth celebrating. Sometimes a given passage of Scripture has a big, bold, and brilliant truth placed next to one that only appears if we pay closer attention. Sometimes we need to rejoice in one while seeking out the other. Psalm 22 is very much like this. A quick first

CHAPTER 3

reading may reveal a grand prophecy of the crucifixion of Christ, but there is more to see if we pay close attention to what comes next. And to get there, we first need to ask a question: What did Jesus mean when he quoted Psalm 22:1?

While our Lord hung on the cross, as the sky darkened and God's wrath against sin was poured out on him, he recited the first line of Psalm 22: "My God, my God, why have you forsaken me?" (Matt. 27:46). What was his purpose in doing so?

It is easy to hear in that exclamation simply a cry of dereliction, a confession of the absence of God's good presence. And, to that interpretation's credit, Jesus certainly felt the unspeakable absence of his Father's pleasure as he suffered on the cross for our sins. This is the grand dark mystery of redemption. We should not brush the horror aside when we think of what Jesus did to save us. However, while that could explain why he cried out, it does not explain why in the moment of his anguish Jesus recited the opening words to this song.

Recognizing that this is the first line of a song is the key to understanding what Jesus meant. As with many songs in your hymnal, it would not be uncommon to refer to a psalm by its opening line, calling to mind the whole psalm.[1] Similarly, even the books of Moses were known in antiquity—and are still known in Judaism today—not by external titles but by a selection of the first few words. In many Western church traditions down to the present day, each psalm is known by its first word or words in Latin, and English literature before the past hundred years is peppered with

---

[1] From the Middle Ages, we have several Jewish manuscripts of the Psalms in Hebrew that, for most psalms, only record the first line. For some psalms, those that would have been sung more often, only the first word is recorded. Presumably, this is a continuation of a tradition where it would have been considered normal to have the whole Psalter memorized, much as you likely have 150 songs you could sing if someone gave you the first line.

references to whole psalms by these introductory words. Jesus's cry as he struggled with the pain of God's judgment against sin was not a cry of desperation. It was a reference to an entire song that, yes, starts in pain and separation from God's felt presence but ends in restoration, vindication, and much more. To understand what Jesus meant, we need to have ears to hear the whole song he began. We need to understand Psalm 22.

Reading Psalm 22

This side of the cross, it is impossible not to read Psalm 22 as about Jesus. It even features (quite rightly) in apologetic arguments, since David vividly describes the scene of the crucifixion a thousand years before it happened. The speaker is mocked and surrounded by enemies, his body is stretched so tightly that his bones are visible enough to be counted, and his internal organs begin to fail. Those who wound him cast lots for his garments and dole them out among themselves. His hands and feet are pierced. He is laid down in the dust of death. Since at least the second century, Christians have pointed to the specific, detailed description of the crucifixion in Psalm 22, claiming it as prophetic proof that Jesus is the Messiah.

That is all right and true. But there is more to be seen here. There are other truths that are often overshadowed by the sheer brilliance of a clear description of Christ's death a millennium before it happened. One should not forget the beauty of the moon just because the sun shines. Our first interest in looking at Psalm 22 in its own right will be to trace the story the psalm tells—not just the story of a righteous person who suffers but of a righteous person who suffers and is vindicated. Then we will do our best to understand who the speaker is.

CHAPTER 3

The Suffering of the Righteous One (Ps. 22:1–21a)

THE SUFFERER'S COMPLAINT (PS. 22:1–2)

To the choirmaster: according to The Doe of the Dawn. A Psalm of David.

> My God, my God, why have you forsaken me?
>> Why are you so far from saving me, from the words of
>>> my groaning?
>
> O my God, I cry by day, but you do not answer,
>> and by night, but I find no rest. (Ps. 22:1–2)

We are met by the familiar words Jesus spoke on the cross, but even in the context of this opening stanza, the cry that seems so desperate is ultimately one of faith in God. He cries out about God's absence not as one finally and fully abandoned but as one who still expects God to answer. He groans; he suffers. He prays to the one who can save him from death, and yet he hears no reply. Unlike some other psalms, there is no hint that the speaker's suffering comes from his own sin or the consequences of his actions. He is in hardship, but he is not at fault. There is nothing that would lead him to suspect anything other than God's kindness and swift response, yet he finds no rest and hears no answer to his groans. He prays for salvation but does not, at first, find it.

THE SUFFERER'S FAITH (PS. 22:3–11)

> Yet you are holy,
>> enthroned on the praises of Israel.
>
> In you our fathers trusted;

> they trusted, and you delivered them.
> To you they cried and were rescued;
> > in you they trusted and were not put to shame.
>
> But I am a worm and not a man,
> > scorned by mankind and despised by the people.
> All who see me mock me;
> > they make mouths at me; they wag their heads;
> "He trusts in the Lord; let him deliver him;
> > let him rescue him, for he delights in him!"
>
> Yet you are he who took me from the womb;
> > you made me trust you at my mother's breasts.
> On you was I cast from my birth,
> > and from my mother's womb you have been my God.
> Be not far from me,
> > for trouble is near,
> > and there is none to help. (Ps. 22:3–11)

Amid his suffering and God's absence, however, the speaker does not doubt God's goodness. He knows that God remains the same yesterday, today, and forever, and so he knows that the same God who saved the fathers can save him. He knows that God remains holy and that those who trust in him are not put to shame.

Yet shame surrounds him. He is an outcast, mocked and hated by all who see him. Something has gone horribly wrong, since the people who see him ridicule him for his faith in God (22:8). In the story this psalm recounts, something has happened that causes everyone around the speaker to believe that he is not in God's favor, that his trust in the Lord is ill-founded. Since they mock him for trusting in the Lord to deliver him, there must be some piece of the story we are missing, something that makes the Lord's deliverance seem implausible to them.

Yet the speaker does not waver in his trust. He knows who God was to the fathers, he knows who God has been to him throughout his life, and so he remains resolute in trusting the Lord who received him from his mother's womb.

THE SUFFERER'S TORMENT (PS. 22:12–18)

> Many bulls encompass me;
>   strong bulls of Bashan surround me;
> they open wide their mouths at me,
>   like a ravening and roaring lion.
>
> I am poured out like water,
>   and all my bones are out of joint;
> my heart is like wax;
>   it is melted within my breast;
> my strength is dried up like a potsherd,
>   and my tongue sticks to my jaws;
>   you lay me in the dust of death.
>
> For dogs encompass me;
>   a company of evildoers encircles me;
> they have pierced my hands and feet—
> I can count all my bones—
> they stare and gloat over me;
> they divide my garments among them,
>   and for my clothing they cast lots. (Ps. 22:12–18)

His faith, however, does not deliver him from suffering. He prays to God for salvation, and God does not spare him. Because of its similarity to the crucifixion, this passage of Psalm 22 often gets the most attention in sermons, debates, and apologetic literature—and deservedly so. The description is so uncannily similar as to be undeniable. After the poetic description of his enemies as ravening beasts, the speaker describes utter physical agony. His body is stretched out so that his joints are separated and his bones countable (Ps. 22:14, 17). His hands and feet are pierced—a detail unique to crucifixion. His clothes are divided and have lots cast for them (Ps. 22:18; cf. Matt. 27:35; Mark 15:24; Luke 23:34; John 19:24, citing Ps. 22:18). People surround him and mock him (Ps. 22:17; cf. Matt. 27:41–44, alluding to Ps. 22:8). He is incredibly thirsty (Ps. 22:15; cf. John 19:28, claiming his thirst was "to fulfill the Scripture"). His heart fails (Ps. 22:14), and he is laid in the ground, dead (Ps. 22:15; cf. Matt. 27:60; Mark 15:46; Luke 23:53; John 19:41–42). This could be read as a metaphorical description of David's experience, but the rest of the psalm's correspondences to Jesus's crucifixion should cause us to look with suspicion at any suggestion that "you lay me in the dust of death" (Ps. 22:15) is merely poetic language. The speaker of Psalm 22 goes down to the dead.

All this raises a question: Who could this be? Although the superscript indicates that this is a psalm of David, certainly by now we suspect that it is merely by him, not about him. David may have been generally righteous (1 Kings 15:4–5), he may have suffered and been despised by his enemies, but when did David experience this?

THE SUFFERER'S PLEA (PS. 22:19–21A)

But you, O Lord, do not be far off!
O you my help, come quickly to my aid!

> Deliver my soul from the sword,
> > my precious life from the power of the dog!
> > Save me from the mouth of the lion! (Ps. 22:19–21a)

And yet the sufferer still speaks. Speaking in vivid imagery, he asks to be saved from the sword, the dog, and the lion. The sword represents death by violence. The dog in Scripture is a carrion animal that scavenges corpses. The lion can be an image either of arrogant, slanderous violence (Ps. 22:13) or of destruction that leaves the victim in pieces (Amos 3:12).

The Vindication of the Righteous One (Ps. 22:21b–24)

> You have rescued me from the horns of the wild oxen!
>
> I will tell of your name to my brothers;
> > in the midst of the congregation I will praise you:
> You who fear the LORD, praise him!
> > All you offspring of Jacob, glorify him,
> > and stand in awe of him, all you offspring of Israel!
> For he has not despised or abhorred
> > the affliction of the afflicted,
> and he has not hidden his face from him,
> > but has heard, when he cried to him. (Ps. 22:21b–24)

In a moment, everything is different. The psalm undergoes an immediate and unexpected reversal. Even the poetic form itself points to how strange and sudden this is. Usually in the psalms, the two or three lines of a verse build on one another. But here, between the first half of 22:21 and the second, everything has changed. God has intervened. The sufferer who cries out about God's absence in the midst of his torment and death suddenly speaks of God's salvation and deliverance. How can this be? The psalm does not tell us.

Psalm 22 is not about a righteous sufferer who goes down to death in the absence of God. Psalm 22 is about a righteous sufferer who goes down to death and then is saved by God with lasting effects. The first thing that the speaker does is declare his intention to praise God in the assembly of his brothers (22:22). Then he calls all God's people to worship, and he proclaims the deliverance of God. Others despised him. His enemies mocked him and brought him down to death. But God has not despised him. The same God who felt so absent in 22:1 has not hidden his face. God did not abandon him, even in his affliction.

The Results of the Righteous One (Ps. 22:25–31)

From you comes my praise in the great congregation;
    my vows I will perform before those who fear him.
The afflicted shall eat and be satisfied;
    those who seek him shall praise the LORD!
    May your hearts live forever!

All the ends of the earth shall remember
    and turn to the LORD,
and all the families of the nations
    shall worship before you.
For kingship belongs to the LORD,
    and he rules over the nations.

All the prosperous of the earth eat and worship;
    before him shall bow all who go down to the dust,
    even the one who could not keep himself alive.

Posterity shall serve him;
>   it shall be told of the Lord to the coming generation;
> they shall come and proclaim his righteousness to a people yet unborn,
>   that he has done it. (Ps. 22:25–31)

The psalm then takes another surprising turn. Until now the story has focused on the experience of the speaker, but it assumes a much wider significance in 22:25–31. The "great congregation"—an expression that in the Psalms and Ezra seems to refer to all, or most of, the gathered people of God—praises the speaker. Other afflicted ones somehow benefit. "All the ends of the earth shall remember" what the Lord did for this one man "and turn to the Lord" (Ps. 22:27). In some way the nations, the Gentiles, all families of the earth, will worship God for this one act of deliverance. And not only during the speaker's time. All generations will hear the story—"that he has done it" (22:31), that God has rescued this righteous sufferer from death.

The Identity of the Righteous One

Unlike Psalms 2 and 8, Psalm 22 is incredibly personal. It narrates the suffering, faith, and vindication of an individual who apparently dies and yet who speaks of God's deliverance and praise redounding to God because of it. Much like the Ethiopian eunuch after reading Isaiah 53, we cannot help but wonder, "About whom, I ask you, does the prophet say this, about himself or about someone else?" (Acts 8:34). Who dies and yet lives to proclaim the goodness of God? Whose vindication is good news to all the nations of the earth? Certainly this is not David.

Jesus himself, of course, provides us the answer. The psalm is about him. He alludes to the whole course of Psalm 22 as he recites its first words on the cross. Yes, he will experience God's absence. Yes, he will suffer crucifixion and death while he is mocked. But that is not all this psalm tells. For those who have ears to hear, Jesus's words on the cross speak to his coming resurrection, his coming vindication, and the coming salvation that will extend to the ends of the earth because of what God will do in raising Jesus from the dead. Psalm 22 is about Jesus.

Reading Hebrews

But is it only *about* Jesus?

That question may be a little unclear, so I will give some context. There are different ways that an Old Testament passage can refer to Jesus. One way is through predictive prophecy—that is, a prophet foretells things that will be true of Jesus. "[She] shall call his name Immanuel" (Isa. 7:14) is an example. Psalm 22 does not seem to be predictive prophecy, since it does not clearly predict but rather narrates a personal experience. Another way an Old Testament passage can refer to Jesus is through "typology," a term that refers to the pattern in history and Scripture where a person, thing, event, or institution (a "type") points forward to something that is greater. Moses is a type of Jesus as covenant mediator. David is a type of Jesus as king. If Psalm 22 is read typologically, when the Spirit inspired David to compose this psalm, he chose wording that would accurately, if poetically, describe his own experiences that at the same time pointed to what Jesus would go through. That is a real option.

The third way is what we saw previously with Psalm 2—that is, the Son of God may be personally speaking to us through the mouth of the prophet. Let us see where the interpretation in Hebrews leads us:

For it was fitting that he, for whom and by whom all things exist, in bringing many sons to glory, should make the founder of their salvation perfect through suffering. For he who sanctifies and those who are sanctified all have one source. That is why he is not ashamed to call them brothers, saying,

"I will tell of your name to my brothers;
   in the midst of the congregation I will sing your praise."
      (Heb. 2:10–12)

Hebrews cites the first full verse after the speaker is rescued, Psalm 22:22, and plainly tells us that this is what Jesus said. The argument of Hebrews at this point is that to help humanity, Jesus had to be made human, united to his people in every way. In particular, to become perfect as the founder of salvation, to become qualified to be the Savior of humanity, Jesus had to suffer. But after he suffers, he gladly embraces as his brothers, his family, all those he saves. Jesus declares the Father's name to his brothers, and he is not ashamed of them. Notice how, in compact form, Hebrews 2:10–12 assumes all of Psalm 22. First suffering, then salvation. The author of Hebrews likely knew that Jesus spoke Psalm 22:1 on the cross. In Hebrews 2:10–12, the author assumes that and continues the story. He makes clear that Psalm 22:1 was not the last word. Jesus also speaks Psalm 22:22. Jesus suffered and felt the absence of God, but God did not ultimately hide his face from Jesus. Jesus rose up from the dust of death. And having risen, having been made perfect as the founder of our salvation, he calls us brothers and proclaims God's wonderous works to us.

This psalm is likely also in the background when Hebrews declares, "In the days of his flesh, Jesus offered up prayers and supplications, with loud cries and tears, to him who was able to save him from death, and he was heard because of his reverence" (Heb. 5:7). Just as in Psalm 22, Jesus cries out for salvation from death, and he is heard—not by being spared from death but by God raising him up from death. The message to all generations remains the same: "He has done it" (Ps. 22:31); God has raised Jesus from the dead.

Reading Psalm 22 Again

God structured King David's life to point forward to the life of Christ. But David was also a prophet (Acts 2:30), and his words in Psalm 22 are not simply typological but are the words of Christ speaking through him (Heb. 2:11–12). Yes, Jesus utters the cry in Psalm 22:1 and recounts the crucifixion scene in 22:12–18, but beyond these obvious connections, the whole psalm contains Jesus's words. Following the guidance of the author of Hebrews, I want to pay particular attention to the family language in the second half of Psalm 22 as we read it again.

As Hebrews points out, Jesus's first words after being delivered are a declaration to his "brothers," who are also called the "congregation" (Ps. 22:22). In 22:23 the people of God are addressed as the "offspring of Jacob" and the "offspring of Israel." Then the "great congregation" moves from hearing the praise of God to praising Jesus himself (22:25). Afterward, we are told that not only will "the ends of the earth . . . turn to the Lord" but also "all the families of the nations shall worship before [the Lord]" (22:27). That idea of worshiping "before" the Lord is significant. They will worship the Lord, but they will do so before him—that is, in congregation around him. This is an image of the nations gathered together as one in the courts of the Lord. They are united not only to God but also to God's people. Then "posterity" or, to translate it more woodenly, "seed" or "offspring" will serve the Lord because of Jesus, and a "coming generation"—future descendants—will hear that God raised Jesus (22:30). "A people yet unborn" will hear of God's righteousness in raising Jesus from the dead (22:31).[2]

The last verses of Psalm 22 are about the Gentile mission, the fulfilment of the promise to Abraham that all the nations of the earth will be blessed in his offspring, Jesus Christ. The repeated family language in the psalm highlights one of the great concerns of Scripture. By removing that which separates man from God, Jesus also removes the barriers between Jew and Gentile, between the alienated and warring factions of humanity (Eph. 2:11–22). All those whom Jesus saves are his brothers, gathered in the great congregation before God (Heb. 2:10–12; 12:22–23). And in Psalm 22, the families of the nations are gathered into this congregation as well. They are made Jesus's brothers. Across time and space and nationality, all who are joined to Christ are joined to one another.

Conclusion

Again, we find Jesus directly speaking to us in the Old Testament. And again, the author to the Hebrews was not arbitrary in understanding these words coming from the mouth of Christ. Jesus on the cross was the first to show us that he, ultimately, is the speaker of Psalm 22. As we saw with Psalm 2, when a text itself creates tensions that no character in its context can resolve, the author to the Hebrews helps us to see that it may be Christ speaking. And because the author recognized the voice of Jesus in the second half of Psalm 22, we are presented with a beautiful picture of the whole arc of the New Testament in a single psalm. We can move

---

[2] We hear in this echoes of the argument in Romans where God's righteousness is displayed in Jesus, who was raised for our justification (Rom. 3:21–22; 4:25).

past the striking depiction of Christ's crucifixion not because it is unimportant but because there is more to see. The psalm has more to say. The next time you read the psalm or sing it in worship, you can do so with the confidence that it is not a crucifixion prophecy shoehorned into an otherwise unrelated psalm. Rather, it tells the whole story of Christ's suffering, his death, his resurrection, and the proclamation of his gospel. In Psalm 22, you hear Jesus, through the mouth of David, speaking what he will do for you when you are joined to him as part of his family, one of whom he is not ashamed (Heb. 2:11).

Discussion Questions

1. What does it mean to be Jesus's family?

2. How does the author to the Hebrews convey that all of Psalm 22 contains Jesus's words?

3. What is the difference between reading something typologically and reading it as Jesus directly speaking?

4. How should we use this psalm in worship?

4

Psalm 40

ONE TECHNIQUE that has served me well in interpreting the Bible is looking for patterns and then looking for where those patterns are intentionally broken. When an author sets up expectations and then chooses not to meet those expectations, it is always a passage pregnant with meaning. This is particularly true for highly formulaic portions of Scripture, like genealogies. While our eyes may be tempted to glaze over at the repeated structures and phrases, the repetition is training us in what to expect and thus highlighting the unexpected. Genesis 5 is punctuated by the phrase, "and he died," so we cannot help but notice Enoch, who does not die. Matthew 1 is full of fathers begetting sons, so whenever a woman is mentioned, she stands out, and Jesus born of Mary stands out most of all because in his case alone no father begets.

This technique also serves us well in the Psalms. While every psalm is its own composition, two types of patterns emerge across the Psalter. The first pattern is genre. Some psalms follow the same general course. Psalms of thanksgiving generally look like one another.

CHAPTER 4

Psalms of repentance generally look like one another. Psalms asking for deliverance generally look like one another. That is not to say that a given psalmist cannot alter the pattern or mix types of psalms; both of these things happen. But it is to say that these general patterns can help us recognize both what a psalm is trying to do and when a pattern is not followed. The second type of pattern that emerges in the psalms is what we can call clusters. There are several groupings of psalms that are clearly meant to be read together. The clearest example of this is the "songs of ascents" (Pss. 120–134). These were meant to be sung together on pilgrimage to Jerusalem and, more or less, narrate the experience of coming from far away to the temple. Another cluster is the "psalms of Asaph" (Pss. 73–83). There are also smaller groupings, where one psalm seems to be a continuation of the one before it (e.g., Pss. 42–43).

I explain this because Psalm 40 could constitute a challenge to the type of reading we have been doing so far in this study. You may read through this psalm and not find any of the tensions we have seen so far in Psalms 2, 8, and 22. And yet, the author to the Hebrews insists that at least one portion of Psalm 40 is spoken by Jesus himself. This may at first seem strange or forced upon the psalm. However, if we pay close attention to patterns, if we see how the psalm works in its own right, we will see the lines along which Hebrews interprets Psalm 40. Jesus does speak here, so much so that when Spurgeon set out his view of the purpose of this psalm, the first words he wrote were, "Jesus is evidently here." Even more directly, when commenting on Psalm 40:6, Spurgeon claimed, "Here we enter upon one of the most wonderful passages in the whole of the Old Testament, a passage in which the incarnate Son of God is seen not through a glass darkly, but as it were face to face."[1] Let us see how we can read the psalm so as to meet him.

Reading Psalm 40

Traditionally, Psalm 40 is seen as the answer to Psalm 39. In Psalm 39, David cries out for deliverance, pleading with God, "Give ear to my cry" (Ps. 39:12). As Psalm 40 begins, David rejoices, "He inclined to me and heard my cry" (Ps. 40:1). David starts with thanksgiving, but somehow the psalm ends backwards, again calling out for deliverance (40:11–17) in words that sound very much like Psalm 70, a request for salvation and for judgment on his enemies. What happened? This break in the usual patterns of psalm composition should cause us to look deeper. The psalm begins in a song of thanksgiving, praising God for answering the pleas of the previous psalm (40:1–5), and the psalm ends completely disjointed from where it began—no longer responding to Psalm 39, no longer delivered, but needing deliverance from enemies (40:11–17). Between these two portions, as if out of nowhere, we find a discussion of sacrifice, scrolls, and God's preparation of a righteous individual (40:6–10).

Thanksgiving (Ps. 40:1–5)

To the choirmaster. A Psalm of David.

> I waited patiently for the LORD;
>   he inclined to me and heard my cry.
> He drew me up from the pit of destruction,
>   out of the miry bog,
> and set my feet upon a rock,

---

1 C. H. Spurgeon, *The Treasury of David* (London: Marshall Brothers, 1869), 2:235.

> making my steps secure.
> He put a new song in my mouth,
>   a song of praise to our God.
> Many will see and fear,
>   and put their trust in the Lord.
>
> Blessed is the man who makes
>   the Lord his trust,
> who does not turn to the proud,
>   to those who go astray after a lie!
> You have multiplied, O Lord my God,
>   your wondrous deeds and your thoughts toward us;
>   none can compare with you!
> I will proclaim and tell of them,
>   yet they are more than can be told. (Ps. 40:1–5)

The opening verses of Psalm 40 are just what we would expect for a psalm of thanksgiving. David recounts waiting for God and receiving God's answer. He is moved from danger and instability to stability and safety (40:2). As is normal in the psalms, this act of deliverance results in praise (40:3). He then turns to the people of God and reflects on how God performs wonderous acts of deliverance not only for himself but also for all who trust in him (40:4–5). God's goodness, kindness, and faithfulness to his people are beyond reckoning, and as David tries to tell of them, he knows he can never recount them all (40:5).

All sense of danger is past. There is no longer any uncertainty. David sings in safety as God has put him far away from the pit of destruction. Also, while David's deliverance will result in praise among the people, it is not like Psalm 22 in which a single act of salvation has effects that go beyond David's life. Rather, this act of deliverance in Psalm 40 is one example of God's innumerable wonderous deeds that he accomplishes for the people. The logic is this: praise God and trust in him. He saved me; he can save you too. We hear not of a singular saving act but of God's consistent pattern of saving those who trust in him (40:4–5).

Obedience (Ps. 40:6–10)

> In sacrifice and offering you have not delighted,
>   but you have given me an open ear.
> Burnt offering and sin offering
>   you have not required.
> Then I said, "Behold, I have come;
>   in the scroll of the book it is written of me:
> I delight to do your will, O my God;
>   your law is within my heart."
>
> I have told the glad news of deliverance
>   in the great congregation;
> behold, I have not restrained my lips,
>   as you know, O Lord.
> I have not hidden your deliverance within my heart;
>   I have spoken of your faithfulness and your salvation;
> I have not concealed your steadfast love and your faithfulness
>   from the great congregation. (Ps. 40:6–10)

The poetry of the Old Testament is often marked by sudden shifts. Without a hint of transition, the speaker changes, the subject shifts, or the grammar of the verbs moves about. Suddenly, Psalm 40 speaks not of salvation but sacrifice.

CHAPTER 4

Some interpreters have tried tracing a logical flow here. Under the Old Testament system, thanksgiving offerings would be appropriate after one was delivered from calamity by God. David knows this but finds them insufficient to express his gratitude for the immeasurable grace of God. While this solution is neat, it does not reflect the text itself. While one of the words David uses—the one translated as "offering"—is appropriate for a thanks offering, that is not all he says. He goes on to specify "burnt offering and sin offering" (Ps. 40:6), and these are not offerings of thanks but of atonement and propitiation. David groups *all* of these together, showing that he is talking not about the insufficiency of a lamb to express the extent of his thanks but rather about all the categories of sacrifice. He views all these sacrifices and says something unprecedented in the Old Testament: God did not desire them or ask for them.

Now, David cannot be saying that Leviticus does not come from God. Such a surface reading is out of bounds because it reads one part of Scripture in contradiction to another. A possible option is to read this along the lines of 1 Samuel 15:22:

And Samuel said,

> "Has the Lord as great delight in burnt offerings and
>   sacrifices,
>   as in obeying the voice of the Lord?
> Behold, to obey is better than sacrifice,
>   and to listen than the fat of rams."

There the distinction is between actually obeying God's word and offering external shows of piety that look obedient but are not.

Something of that idea is likely present in Psalm 40:6, but that still does not do full justice to David's words. He does not say, "You have delighted less," or "You require these sacrifices less." Instead he says, "You have not delighted" in them, and "You have not required" them. There must be something more here. We may not be able to resolve it with the psalm alone, but for now we can say that God has revealed to David that there is some insufficiency in the sacrifices, the very sacrifices that God instituted.

The enigmatic quality of this portion of the psalm only grows with the next verse. The speaker, whom God has given "an open ear" (40:6; more on this later), comes forward with a scroll of a book that speaks about him. The law of God, presumably the same law that speaks of the sacrifices, is in the heart of the speaker, and God's will is his delight (40:8; the same verb used to say that God has "not delighted" in the sacrifices in 40:6).

In the following verses, the obedient speaker's delight in God's will and law is demonstrated as he declares God's faithfulness and deliverance to the great congregation. The speaker is emphatic through his use of negatives: "I have not restrained," "I have not hidden," "I have not concealed" (40:9–10). The speaker's mission, the thing for which he has come, is to proclaim God's steadfast love and faithfulness, his salvation and deliverance, to the great congregation. Perhaps we hear in this some echoes of Psalm 22.

Petition (Ps. 40:11–17)

> As for you, O LORD, you will not restrain
>   your mercy from me;
> your steadfast love and your faithfulness will
>   ever preserve me!

For evils have encompassed me
>   beyond number;
> my iniquities have overtaken me,
>   and I cannot see;
> they are more than the hairs of my head;
>   my heart fails me.
>
> Be pleased, O Lord, to deliver me!
>   O Lord, make haste to help me!
> Let those be put to shame and disappointed altogether
>   who seek to snatch away my life;
> let those be turned back and brought to dishonor
>   who delight in my hurt!
> Let those be appalled because of their shame
>   who say to me, "Aha, Aha!"
>
> But may all who seek you
>   rejoice and be glad in you;
> may those who love your salvation
>   say continually, "Great is the Lord!"
> As for me, I am poor and needy,
>   but the Lord takes thought for me.
> You are my help and my deliverer;
>   do not delay, O my God! (Ps. 40:11–17)

Once again, everything has changed. Far from being a fully righteous representative of God in the great assembly who has the law in his heart, the speaker is beset by evils without and within. The innumerable goodnesses of God to his people are replaced by the speaker's iniquities, which are more than the hairs on his head (40:12). The speaker is both in dire need of salvation and knows that he will be saved. He has enemies who wish to destroy and shame him, but he knows that he will experience the gladness of God's salvation. What makes this section stand out is the intermingling of confidence and request. Even as his life is in danger, he knows that God will deliver him. Even as he is brought down low, he knows that the Lord will raise him up.

Reading Hebrews

The argument of the epistle to the Hebrews advances by examining passages of the Old Testament in order to compare individuals and institutions to Jesus. Over the course of his argument, the author shows how Jesus is better than these Old Testament examples and how the Old Testament itself consistently points to a time when its institutions will fade away in light of the perfection that comes in Christ. At the beginning of Hebrews 10, the author is comparing the Levitical sacrifices, particularly the once-a-year sacrifice of the Day of Atonement, to the once-for-all sacrifice of Jesus. Reflecting on those Levitical sacrifices, he says,

> But in these sacrifices there is a reminder of sins every year. For it is impossible for the blood of bulls and goats to take away sins.
> Consequently, when Christ came into the world, he said,
>
> "Sacrifices and offerings you have not desired,
>   but a body have you prepared for me;
> in burnt offerings and sin offerings
>   you have taken no pleasure.
> Then I said, 'Behold, I have come to do your will, O God,
>   as it is written of me in the scroll of the book.'"

When he said above, "You have neither desired nor taken pleasure in sacrifices and offerings and burnt offerings and sin offerings" (these are offered according to the law), then he added, "Behold, I have come to do your will." He does away with the first in order to establish the second. And by that will we have been sanctified through the offering of the body of Jesus Christ once for all. (Heb. 10:3–10)

For our purposes, there are two things we must observe about the author's treatment of Psalm 40. First, the author says that Jesus spoke these words "when Christ came into the world" (Heb. 10:5)—that is, at his incarnation. Obviously, Jesus could not have said these words within Mary's womb or as an infant, so the author means that Jesus spoke these words through David as a prophet and that they are spoken from the perspective of the moment of the incarnation. Second, the author to the Hebrews views the quotation of Psalm 40 as containing a sequence of events: first the statement that God does not take pleasure in the Levitical sacrifices followed by the statement that Jesus has come to do the will of God. This sequence, then, reveals a change in God's relationship to humanity. The Levitical offerings that cannot make people perfectly holy are set aside, and the offering of Jesus that does sanctify people is established.

Before we move on, we should note the difference that you may have noticed between Psalm 40:6 and its quotation in Hebrews. Psalm 40:6 reads, "You have given me an open ear." This translates the Hebrew clause that woodenly reads, "Ears you have dug for me." The author of Hebrews quotes it as "a body have you prepared for me" (Heb. 10:5), which agrees with the oldest manuscripts we have of the Greek translation of the Psalms. While scholars debate how the Greek Psalms ended up with this translation, the most likely explanation is that the Greek renders what was meant by the Hebrew. "Ears you have dug for me" is a strange phrase no matter which language it appears in. It likely means that God has made it possible for me to hear and obey his word. It is not far from there to reach the clarifying translation, "a body have you prepared for me"—that is, you have given me what I need to do your will. No translation perfectly matches the language it translates, and that is just as true here as it is for any modern work. Significantly, while the church has historically seen "a body have you prepared for me" as a clear reference to the incarnation, Hebrews does not rely on that interpretation for its argument. Rather, the author focuses on the coming of the one written in the book to do the will of God as a replacement for the Levitical sacrifices.

Reading Psalm 40 Again

How does the treatment of Psalm 40 in Hebrews help us better understand this psalm of shifting stories? Why does the pattern break as it does? As we saw when we first read Psalm 40, the transitions to and away from the middle section are the most confusing. From a context of deliverance, we move to a discussion of the insufficiency of sacrifices and of the foretold arrival of a perfectly righteous representative of God who does God's will and proclaims his goodness. Then, without any clear change—all in the first person—the speaker is suddenly drowning in afflictions without and sins within, though he is unshakably confident that God will deliver him. The use of Psalm 40:6–8 in Hebrews provides the key: in the middle portion of Psalm 40, Jesus himself speaks; in the first and last portions, he does not.

The first portion of the psalm, the thanksgiving for deliverance, is clearly David speaking. Yet even this is not so simple. This is not a historical book but a psalm. David speaks, and the people of God echo his voice. We sing the psalm, thanking God for delivering us and calling out to those around us that, because of God's unending goodness toward his people, he will deliver them too.

But how can we say such a thing? How do we know that he will fully deliver? How do we know that there is a lasting salvation for us? It cannot be because of our deeds, and it cannot be because of the sacrifices offered day in and day out, year after year. As assurance of God's never-ending deliverance, Jesus speaks. He sets aside the Levitical sacrifices, ordained by God as they were, and sets out what they pointed to all along: the arrival of Jesus in the flesh. He declares that he has come to do the will of God and offer himself, establishing an eternal salvation. The book, the very law that commanded the sacrifices, speaks about him. Though his arrival is new, his coming forth is of old. Having done the will of God in the sacrifice of himself, he proclaims this good news to the people. He announces to all God's gathered people the faithfulness of God and his own faithfulness to not shrink back.

But who is speaking at the end of the psalm? There are different ways of answering this that amount to the same thing. First, one can say that Christ continues to speak but now on behalf of his people—that is, he speaks as our representative. He is our head, so he can speak for his body. He has borne our iniquities, so he can give us words to pray when we are faced by the overwhelming tide of our sins. The second option is to say that these are the words of the believer, the member of Christ's body. We have been saved, and we will certainly be saved. But we are currently beset by external evils and our own sins. Note again the mixture of certainty and pleas. Often in the Psalms, the psalmist is confident on the basis of his righteousness (e.g., Pss. 7:8; 18:20, 24; 26:11), or he desperately pleads for mercy in awareness of his sins (e.g., Pss. 38, 51).

Here we find a strange gospel mixture. Precisely in the awareness of the extent of his sins, as he feels them more numerous than the hairs on his head, the psalmist knows God will deliver him. This can only be said by someone who understands the great salvation accomplished and proclaimed by Christ in Psalm 40:6–10. Because Jesus has done God's will, because Jesus has replaced the repeated and ineffectual sacrifices with the all-perfecting sacrifice of himself, you and I can say, even as we are confronted with our sins,

> As for you, O LORD, you will not restrain
>   your mercy from me;
> your steadfast love and your faithfulness
>   will ever preserve me! (Ps. 40:11)

Conclusion

Psalm 40 is a gospel psalm. The shifting pattern of speakers, the change from salvation to an ongoing need for deliverance, and the intrusion of one who obeys and proclaims God's will are only understandable in light of the relationship between Christ and his church. In Jesus, God delivers us so securely that we will never slip (40:1–5). The offerings of the Levitical system pale in comparison to the offering made by the Son of God. In Jesus's life, death, and resurrection, he saves to the uttermost those who come to God through him. And he proclaims this message of salvation to the great congregation, his people throughout the world (40:6–10). In Jesus, God's people know that no matter their sins or the dangers they face, their redemption is secure and their deliverance is coming (40:11–17). In Jesus, your sins do not separate you from God any more. There is no danger that the solid rock he has set you on will crumble. If your iniquities are as many as the hairs on your head, even still you can know that he will not keep his mercy from you.

Discussion Questions

1. According to Psalm 40, what did Jesus come to do?

2. How does "the scroll of the book" talk about Jesus?

3. How does Psalm 40 reflect your experience?

4. How does Psalm 40 itself point to the interpretation that Hebrews provides?

5

Psalm 45

THE THING ABOUT CLICHÉS is that they reveal striking truths.

To say that your beloved's eyes are like the stars may sound trite (and it may be unforgivable in poetry), but it captures that moment when you look at the one you love and see something that cannot be adequately explained by this sublunary world. To call young children "little angels" is often mere sentimentality, but it can also express the innocence of children and their sheer enjoyment in the created world, the wonder and seriousness and self-forgetfulness with which they go about their toddling days.

So it is with the word "breathtaking."

Like most clichés, the term seemed to me an exaggeration, simply a synonym for "very beautiful." Until my wedding day. As the music played, my soon-to-be wife turned a corner, came into view, and for a moment my breath caught in my chest. It actually happened. I had seen her before. I had even seen her earlier that day as we went about our preparations. But seeing her then, that woman in that place for that purpose, moved me like no sight ever has before or since. "Very beautiful" simply does not do the job.

CHAPTER 5

In Psalm 45, we also find ourselves at a wedding. And in the psalmist's poetic inspiration, "very beautiful" again does not do the job. Superlatives and lavish descriptions of glory and power multiply. This is a wedding unlike any other before or since. And in this wedding, it is not the bride who captures every eye but the groom. The psalm is clear: he is breathtaking.

Reading Psalm 45

There is only one love song in the Psalter. There is only one psalm where the psalmist expresses his intention to compose the psalm before jumping into his theme. There is only one psalm where the psalmist builds anticipation by speaking of how pleasing his topic is and how ready he is to sing before actually beginning the song. Psalm 45 stands apart, drawing our attention and piquing our curiosity. Who is this king? Why a song quite like this? Whose wedding is this?

The psalmist gradually unfolds this song of praise, but unlike other songs in the Psalter, Psalm 45 does not recount God's acts of deliverance. This is no psalm of the exodus or of deliverance from danger. It does not consider the grandness of creation or the intimate knitting of human life in the womb. Rather, the psalmist bursts into pleasing praises of a king on a throne and his queen. A wedding makes the psalmist a ready scribe, eager to transcribe the splendors he sees.

Why should this be? Is this out of place? Why use language of extravagant praise—language elsewhere in the Scriptures reserved for God alone—to describe this man who rides out to claim his bride? Psalm 45 conducts us into this mystery and shows us the king in his beauty, the king on his throne, and, in her turn, the queen in her beauty. No names are given. No clear historical reference points are mentioned. But as we are ushered into the presence of this man who is more than a man, we find ourselves in the very heart of the central story of the Scriptures.

The King in His Beauty (Ps. 45:1–5)

To the choirmaster: according to Lilies. A Maskil of the Sons of Korah; a love song.

> My heart overflows with a pleasing theme;
>> I address my verses to the king;
>> my tongue is like the pen of a ready scribe.
>
> You are the most handsome of the sons of men;
>> grace is poured upon your lips;
>> therefore God has blessed you forever.
>
> Gird your sword on your thigh, O mighty one,
>> in your splendor and majesty!
>
> In your majesty ride out victoriously
>> for the cause of truth and meekness and righteousness;
>> let your right hand teach you awesome deeds!
>
> Your arrows are sharp
>> in the heart of the king's enemies;
>> the peoples fall under you. (Ps. 45:1–5)

This king stands above all others. The psalmist extols his excellence. We learn that he is more beautiful than any other man, his words are skilled and right, and he is majestic in power.

It is likely that many of us need to push through a sense of awkwardness in reading this psalm. We are not used to love songs about how handsome a man is. It is made even stranger by the fact that it was written by other men, "the Sons of Korah." We are comfortable reading of his strength for battle, but we pause reading about his beauty.

Yet both his strength and his beauty are necessary. Although the ancient world was more frank about exclamations of male physical excellence, even that observation misses the point. This king's beauty is for his bride. The more excellent he is in every way, the better he is for his bride, and the more significant this wedding becomes. This isn't the wedding of a normal man seen through the eyes of love but the wedding of the greatest man. He is beautiful in appearance, gracious in his words, and majestic in might. He rides in victorious conquest, putting all war to rest.

But there's even more! His strength is not simply the assertion of power. This is no petty tyrant. His arrows are sharp, but they fly "for the cause of truth and meekness and righteousness" (Ps. 45:4). By his strength, lies are exposed and the meek inherit the earth. In him, we do not see the old lie about might making right; rather his strength is displayed in the cause of all that is right.

The King on His Throne (Ps. 45:6–9)

> Your throne, O God, is forever and ever.
>   The scepter of your kingdom is a scepter of
>   uprightness;
>   you have loved righteousness and hated wickedness.
> Therefore God, your God, has anointed you
>   with the oil of gladness beyond your companions;
>   your robes are all fragrant with myrrh and aloes and
>   cassia.
> From ivory palaces stringed instruments make you glad;

> daughters of kings are among your ladies of honor;
> at your right hand stands the queen in gold of Ophir.
> (Ps. 45:6–9)

Suddenly, our understanding of this man changes. The most handsome among men is God with an eternal throne (45:6). And yet, God has a God (45:7). Do not let the disorienting nature of this revelation cause you to skip over what is going on. We must still be talking about the man who is to be married; 45:8–9 picks up this theme again with the wedding party in full regalia. And yet, without blushing or hedging, the psalmist describes this royal groom in terms only suited to God. He is directly called "God." His throne is not merely great but lasts forever and ever. He rules with the rod of righteousness.

To understand this in terms of the Old Testament alone is difficult if not impossible. Many interpreters, refusing to accept that the psalm means exactly what it says, have seen this as an exaggerated description of a human king. After all, another psalm speaks of humans as "gods" (Ps. 82:6). Even John Calvin treats the "literal" sense of Psalm 45 as about Solomon, though with clear typological resonances with Christ.[1] Yet it is wholly inappropriate to refer to a mere human as "God" without qualification, and no other passage of the Old Testament approaches anything like this. If Solomon is here at all, he is wearing someone else's clothes, simply a frame to hang words on that describe someone else, someone greater.

I want to suggest that we avoid attributing this psalm to Solomon's wedding, that we resist the urge to find an Old Testament

---

1   John Calvin, *Commentary on the Book of Psalms*, trans. James Anderson (Grand Rapids, MI: Eerdmans, 1949), 2:173–76.

figure this psalm could slightly resemble if we squint hard enough. Let the psalm speak for itself. After all, why can a psalmist not also be a prophet?

There is a king who is to be married. He is beautiful and glorious. He is certainly human since he is compared with the other "sons of men" (45:2) and has companions (45:7). And yet, the psalmist straightforwardly calls him "God" (45:6)—a unique occurrence in the Old Testament. Thus, we see a man who is God, who also exists in relationship *to* God. That is, God has a God who rewards him for the wonderful things he does as a man. This reward includes being "anointed" (Greek *echrisen*; note the appearance of "Christ" language) "with the oil of gladness" (45:7)—that is, he is made supremely happy.

This happy king—who somehow is both God and man and also blessed by God—is precisely the one who is to be married. He stands in all his finery, adorned with myrrh and other fine fragrances, accompanied by music on stringed instruments, flanked by attendants, and in the presence of his bride, the queen.

The Queen in Her Beauty (Ps. 45:10–17)

> Hear, O daughter, and consider, and incline your ear:
>   forget your people and your father's house,
>   and the king will desire your beauty.
> Since he is your lord, bow to him.
>   The people of Tyre will seek your favor with gifts,
>   the richest of the people.
>
> All glorious is the princess in her chamber, with robes
>   interwoven with gold.
>   In many-colored robes she is led to the king,

> with her virgin companions following behind her.
> With joy and gladness they are led along
> > as they enter the palace of the king.
>
> In place of your fathers shall be your sons;
> > you will make them princes in all the earth.
> I will cause your name to be remembered in all
> > generations;
> > therefore nations will praise you forever and ever.
> > (Ps. 45:10–17)

The psalmist turns and addresses the bride as she approaches her wedding day. Even couples that are madly in love with one another can have cold feet in the run up to the wedding, and the psalmist takes advantage of this common experience to address the bride with some fatherly counsel.

Instead of worrying or fearing over the newness of this marriage, the bride is advised to forget what lies behind and to look forward to what lies ahead. All that is past is prologue; the main story now begins. In place of what went before, expressed as "your people and your father's house" (45:10) and "your fathers" (45:16), the bride is called to look forward to the king himself, to her own beauty in the king's retinue, and to the future this marriage will bring.

The king himself has power and authority: he is "lord" (45:11). And yet he does not keep this power to himself but shares it with his queen. Because his desire is for her, he shares his rule with her, and the nations will seek *her* favor (45:12). She becomes mighty in the might of her king.

She also becomes beautiful. In cloth-of-gold and many-colored robes, with attendants flanking her in splendor, she walks within the palace and company of the king. To be in the presence of the queen strikes joy in the hearts of those who accompany her (45:15). Her splendor radiates in the faces of those who see her. And it is in this beauty that she is brought to the king. The wedding—long awaited, long anticipated—finally occurs. In the palace of the king, in his house and in his presence, she takes her place.

And, as is naturally the case, children will follow. For all generations, her sons shall be princes. Do not be misled by the translation here. Modern English speakers hear "prince" and think merely of the child of a monarch. That is, we do not imagine princes as rulers but as waiting in luxury to maybe someday become king. The word translated "prince" is broader and stronger than this, however. While sometimes it is synonymous with "king," more often it refers to the leader over a specific group or someone with delegated authority. These princes are not hapless princelings in the palace but those who also share in the authority of the king. They rule. They govern. For all time, and to the praise of their mother the queen, they will rule well in the earth.

Reading Hebrews

In the grand chain of Old Testament passages comparing Jesus to the angels in Hebrews 1, the author goes to great pains to show that Jesus is better than the angels in essence, in titles, in power, and in stability. The angels are mutable; they change to suit God's purposes for them. The Son, however, is stable. When we look at Psalm 102 later in this book, we will see how the Son is stable in his essence, in who he is. In the citation of Psalm 45 in Hebrews 1, however, we find the author emphasizing that the Son is stable in his *reign*.

Of the angels he says,

> "He makes his angels winds,
> and his ministers a flame of fire."

But of the Son he says,

> "Your throne, O God, is forever and ever,
> the scepter of uprightness is the scepter of your kingdom.
> You have loved righteousness and hated wickedness;
> therefore God, your God, has anointed you
> with the oil of gladness beyond your companions."
> (Heb. 1:7–9)

The author presents the text of the psalm without further comment, leading us to infer the significance from the contrast. The angels may be changed as God sends them to minister, but the Son reigns on an eternal throne. He does not change or waver, nor is he appointed for a temporary purpose. Furthermore, the author of Hebrews is clear: the angels are ministering spirits, created beings that God can change. The Son, however, *is* God.

Do not skip over this. The author of Hebrews presents the psalmist directly addressing Jesus as God. Even more, did you notice who the "he" is as the quote is introduced? "But of the Son *he* says" (Heb. 1:8). Who is the one who calls the Son "God"? To determine this, we need to go back to 1:5: "For to which of the angels did God ever say?" God speaks the psalms in Hebrews 1. Thus, in 1:8, God the Father addresses the Son as God, even as he declares that the Son can call the Father his God in 1:9. The divinity of Christ and the relations between the members of the Trinity are not foreign concepts imposed on the Bible but rather are clearly proclaimed in the pages of Scripture, not least here in Hebrews.

In the argumentation of Hebrews, this passage is about the incarnate and exalted Son. We find in Hebrews 1:3 that after accomplishing purification through his atoning work, he sat down at the right hand of the Father's majesty. It is there, as the incarnate, resurrected, glorified God-man that Jesus now sits on the throne of heaven. This is not to say that there was ever a time when the divine Son of God did not rule over creation but that now his assumed humanity is raised up to its rightful place.

We can know that the author's use of this psalm features the exalted Jesus because of what he includes. This God has a God who has anointed him because of his love of righteousness and his hatred of wickedness. Because of his accomplishments and righteous life, he has been enthroned and made glad. These statements would be improper if we were talking about things that have been eternally true of God the Son. But they fit the Scripture's story of the Son of God who, though possessing every divine prerogative, emptied himself by adding humanity, lived perfectly, died for his people, rose from the dead, and ascended to heaven in the highest glory.

At this point you might notice that this story—the pattern of incarnation, life, death, resurrection, and glory—keeps popping up. The Psalms keep leading us here. Hebrews keeps leading us here. This is because all of Scripture leads us here. Whether we're looking at a single psalm or the whole sweep of divine revelation, we find the pattern of the life of Christ woven into the fabric of Scripture. We cannot get away from it, and we cannot fully understand any book without it.

So what does Hebrews add to our understanding of the psalm? It makes explicit that the King of Psalm 45 is the Son. Jesus is the human King who is also God. He is the righteous conqueror who is mighty and who speaks grace. And he is getting married.

Reading Psalm 45 Again

As we saw when reading Psalm 45 the first time, it is nearly impossible to read it without reference to Christ. On this side of the new covenant, how can one hear of a king who is God, who conquers in righteousness and has an eternal throne, without thinking of Jesus? And rightly so. This psalm is about him—not about another king that somewhat corresponds to him. The psalmist was a prophet who wrote a song for the wedding of the Son of God. Or, according to Hebrews, through the psalmist God sang of the wedding of his own Son.

One question I avoided earlier in this chapter, however, now needs to be addressed. Who is the bride? Now that we know who the royal groom is, the answer should be obvious: the church. The church is repeatedly depicted as the bride of Christ (see Eph. 5:25–32; Rev. 21:9–22:17), and the people of God in the Old Testament are also described as God's (often unfaithful) bride (Isa. 62:5; Ezek. 23; Hos. 2–4).

This is not some fanciful, strained reading of the psalm but rather where the story of the psalm and of all Scripture leads us. The King who is also God has won for himself a bride. She must leave her former people and life, accept the love of the King, and acknowledge him as Lord. In turn, she will become great and glorious, receiving from him beautiful garments and a share in his power. Yes, these things are spoken in images. The church is not literally a woman who is a queen. But the images do speak.

You, Christian, are a member of this church. You are included in the praise of this bride. The King—the greatest among men and incomparable in beauty—has set his love on you. All strength is in his arm. All beauty is in his appearance. All grace is in his speech. There is no desire you have that does not find its fulfillment in him.

You (united with the church as one) are to be married, and the King you are to marry is God. He will love you with a love as unending as his reign. He will clothe you in the beautiful garments of righteousness. He will make you great and glorious for all time. Why would you look back to the lesser things you left behind to draw near to him? Forget them all and press forward into the wonders of his love for you. Press on until the day that this long awaited wedding finally takes place.

You are also the posterity promised. This King offers crowns to his faithful sons. He shares his strength. He has companions who enter into joy with him. He tells us that when he returns we will rule with him (2 Tim. 2:12; Rev. 20:6). An eternity of glory and rule lie ahead for God's saints. He will make his children princes. We can live now as more than conquerors, demonstrating righteousness in the power he provides, so that we can expect the reward of good and faithful servants who will be raised to rule over cities.

Let me offer a concluding reflection. While the roles this psalm presents to God's people are gendered—a bride to marry Christ the King and sons to be made princes under him—and while these images may appeal more strongly along gender lines, they are true about the church as a whole. On average, men may be more motivated by the promise of ruling beside Christ in power, sharing in his strength. On average, women may be more motivated by the promise of the love of the eternal King, sharing in his beauty. There is a fitness in this. Our common devotion to God as Christians will inevitably express itself in ways that suit both our common humanity and the two unique ways of being human that God has made: male and female.

At the same time, men and women in Christ share a common lot in these things. We will all be wed to the King. He will love us, and we will be satisfied in his beauty. We will all rule with him, exercising dominion over the created order that we were made for as God's image bearers. All Christians together are his bride. All Christians are his sons. What we are in relation to one another is real and good and given by God. What we are in relation to him, what we will find in his resurrection life, is greater even than these.

Conclusion

History is moving toward a wedding. Psalm 45, this enigmatic love song of the Psalter, takes us to the wedding day of the greatest King to ever walk the earth. He is strong, beautiful, gracious, and conquering. King Jesus will rule creation in his resurrected splendor, and this psalm announces the day when he goes forth to claim his bride. He offers beauty, power, and posterity to his queen, who will share in his rule for all time. And, as the psalm unfolds and tells the story of Scripture, we find that we are in the song. We are the King's beloved. Psalm 45 presents us with our wedding day, when we will be forever joined to the glad and powerful presence of Jesus, our Savior and our God. And he, forever, will take our breath away.

Discussion Questions

1. Jesus is described in Psalm 45 as supremely beautiful. How should his beauty shape our desires?

2. How does the future of God's people—sharing in Christ's beauty and authority—affect the way we live today?

3. Christ's love for us is often described with the language of marriage. What does it mean to be part of the bride of Christ?

6

Psalm 95

IT WOULD BE GENEROUS to say that I am inconsistent with family devotions. For me, reading the Bible has always been an individual thing, not a thing that is easily done in a group. I can teach, and I can learn, but it has always felt unnatural to *read with* someone else. Reading for me is something done in isolation, preferably with a good cup of coffee and silence all around. I can talk about a book all day long with other people who have already read it. But reading *with* other people feels strange to me. This likely reveals some profound lack in my own character, but it remains how things currently are.

Because of this, on the rare occasions I have tried reading the Bible with my family as a set we-are-doing-this thing, two things have been true. First, the practice runs out of steam fast. Second, I reach for familiar passages that have long track records of being read together.

Most recently, I attempted Psalm 95. Psalm 95 is part of the daily morning prayer of large branches of Christianity. Historically, it featured in the morning prayers, or *matins*, of the Latin speaking church, and today it still holds that place in Catholicism. Beyond that, in the Anglican tradition, at least the first half of Psalm 95 features as a regular component of the morning prayers and readings.

So I began reading Psalm 95 while my toddler squirmed at the table. Things started off alright but became slightly awkward as I finished the reading:

> Therefore I swore in my wrath,
>   "They shall not enter my rest." (Ps. 95:11)

After a moment of mostly silence—again, a toddler was present, so the silence could not be perfect—my wife commented that she always wondered why that psalm ended so negatively. It always catches you off guard.

And she was right. It does! The psalm begins positively, calling people to worship God together. This is why it is used in so many morning prayers. What better way to start the day than calling one another to worship the Lord? And yet, it ends seemingly in a note of failure. The promise is unobtained and the people are cast off. None enter rest. Why does it end here? Why this sudden voice of warning and judgment? How are we to relate to a psalm that begins in joyful worship and ends in judgment?

With help from Hebrews, we shall see. My hope is that this chapter helps us no longer be caught off guard by Psalm 95.

Reading Psalm 95

Psalm 95 is a song of contrasts. It begins with a grand, sweeping call to worship the Lord in light of his universal sovereignty. He has made all things. All creation is his. We ourselves are his. It ends in the wilderness, meditating on the failures of the generation led out of Egypt by Moses. It is a psalm of the universal and of the particular. It is a psalm of worship and of failure to worship. It is a psalm of redemption and of the rejection of that redemption. And perhaps, as we shall see, it is a psalm of yet more grace to come.

Call to Worship (Ps. 95:1–7a)

> Oh come, let us sing to the LORD;
>   let us make a joyful noise to the rock of our salvation!
> Let us come into his presence with thanksgiving;
>   let us make a joyful noise to him with songs of praise!
> For the LORD is a great God,
>   and a great King above all gods.
> In his hand are the depths of the earth;
>   the heights of the mountains are his also.
> The sea is his, for he made it,
>   and his hands formed the dry land.
>
> Oh come, let us worship and bow down;
>   let us kneel before the LORD, our Maker!
> For he is our God,
>   and we are the people of his pasture,
>   and the sheep of his hand. (Ps. 95:1–7a)

The psalmist calls the people of God to worship. In song and in gladness, with thankfulness in our hearts and on our lips, we are to praise the Lord. As is common in the Psalms, this call to praise is accompanied by reasons. Praise is not an arbitrary obligation but, rather, the response to seeing God for who he is and what he has done for us.

CHAPTER 6

In Psalm 95, the call to worship springs from seeing God as King, Creator, and shepherd. The psalmist starts with praising God as God,

> For the LORD is a great God,
>   and a great King above all gods. (Ps 95:3)

When we praise God, sing songs, offer prayers, or speak of him to others, we are not dealing with mere words. God is not a collection of impressions on our emotions nor a set of lofty ideas. He is not a conceived system or a crafted image. He is a great God. He is really and truly there—supreme over all.

He is "a great King above all gods" (95:3). Every spiritual being in splendor bows before him. No mighty angel or burning seraph can stand apart from God's rule. He is above anything that we prize in our lives or in the universe. He is greater than all and rules all. That he is God and King declares both his majesty and his power. He not only is above all but also reigns over all. His power tells all things how far they may go and what they must do. His authority is absolute in heaven and on the earth.

From "the depths of the earth" to "the heights of the mountains," all things are in his hand (95:4). First, note the contrast. This is a poetic way of expressing "everywhere." Go lower than low, and God rules there. Go higher than high, and still everything is within his hand. The unsearchable depths of the earth and the unscalable heights of the mountains are not far to God. He does not need to strain his reach to rule there. If this psalm were written using modern terms, the psalmist might speak of the far reaches of space. The depth of a black hole's gravity well and the height of the most distant star are both within his hand. (This is less poetic but not less true.)

And all these reaches, heights and depths, are within his *hand*. While certainly this is an image of his control, of God's limitless power, it may indeed be more than that. We know that the hand of the Lord is not only an exercise of power but of care. All things are held by him. Height and depth rest in his palm. The grand expanse of the cosmos is small to the Lord, but he carries it always before him. His power encompasses everything everywhere, but so too does his care. He sustains all things. "In him all things hold together" (Col. 1:17). Nowhere is too far for his power to reach. Nowhere is too far for his loving care to go. After all, this great God and King is also "the rock of our salvation" (Ps. 95:1).

His rule is so near to all because he is the Creator of all. In another contrast, the psalmist declares,

> The sea is his, for he made it,
>   and his hands formed the dry land. (Ps. 95:5)

Reaching back to the third day of Genesis 1, the psalmist reminds us that God made the whole world we inhabit. Before the invention of flight, human life was spent on one of two surfaces: the sea or the land. Whether the shifting seas or the solid land beneath our feet, the Lord God made it. And because he is King (Ps. 95:3), we know that he rules over it with boundless authority, and the psalmist moves us to praise God as both Creator and possessor of the world.

God made all things. He owns them not only by right of power but also by right of creation. All things are his in the deepest sense, since they owe their very being to his word. Without help, without material or tools, God spoke everything into existence. The land we walk and the seas we sail, every reality on which we depend, any substance we can see or touch—God made it all. He is no stranger to anything on earth. Nothing in the vast unexplored seas can surprise him. He is near to all, because he has made all. His power is on display in the very existence of things. Every rock and wave, every valley of the earth and swell of the sea, testifies to the creative power of God.

And we ourselves testify to this. We should bow down and praise God not only because he has made the sea and the land but because he is "our Maker" (95:6). The psalmist moves his eye a bit further down in Genesis 1 and declares the wonderous truth that God made us. He made us intentionally, in his image, and with purpose. We humans are not accidents, not some cosmic unlikelihoods generated by an uncaring universe. We are made. We receive our being from the God who reigns supreme and cares for us.

For Christians, we are doubly his. He created us, and he has made us to be his special people:

> For he is our God,
>   and we are the people of his pasture,
>   and the sheep of his hand. (Ps. 95:7a)

The God who rules over us as King with rights over us as Creator cares for us as a shepherd. He walks with us. He leads us to pleasant places. He watches over us. He feeds us from his hand.

The Scriptures are full of images of good shepherds who spend night and day with their sheep, who lose sleep and watch over them at all times and through all dangers. God is such a shepherd to us. He never abandons, never forsakes. He is never distracted or called away by other duties. He knows all the sheep of his hand and will guide and protect them with the same hand that holds all heights and depths.

Call to Obedience (Ps. 95:7b–11)

> Today, if you hear his voice,
> > do not harden your hearts, as at Meribah,
> > as on the day at Massah in the wilderness,
> when your fathers put me to the test
> > and put me to the proof, though they had seen my work.
> For forty years I loathed that generation
> > and said, "They are a people who go astray in their heart,
> > and they have not known my ways."
> Therefore I swore in my wrath,
> > "They shall not enter my rest." (Ps. 95:7b–11)

At this point, the psalm takes a dramatic turn. Genesis gives way to Exodus. The God who created all, who shepherds his people, who is the very rock of salvation, is rejected by his own people even as he led them out of danger and into safety. The psalmist calls to everyone who hears his song,

> Today, if you hear his voice,
> > do not harden your hearts. (95:7b–8)

There is a danger that faces everyone who comes to praise the Lord. Your heart might harden against him, even in the face of his wonderous works for you.

The references to Massah and Meribah recall the story of Exodus 17:1–7. Shortly after being redeemed from slavery in Egypt and crossing the Red Sea, the people of Israel began to complain. First they complained about food, and God gave them manna. Then, in Exodus 17, they complained again—this time about a lack of water. While all the details are not given, this complaint seems to have been even more contentious. They fought with Moses (Ex. 17:2) in addition to grumbling against him (17:3). Moses recognized that this quarrel was not merely directed at him but was an attempt to test God (Ex. 17:2)—that is, an expression of doubt in his goodness and good purposes for them. Subsequently, God miraculously provided water from a rock through Moses, and we are told that Moses "called the name of the place Massah and Meribah, because of the quarreling of the people of Israel, and because they tested the Lord by saying, 'Is the Lord among us or not?'" (Ex. 17:7). In their quarreling and complaining, the people ultimately doubted whether the Lord was really with them.

This, then, set a pattern where the people repeatedly doubted God's shepherding of them, rejecting his ways in favor of their own. They made an idol of a golden calf, grumbled constantly against God, and rejected the promised land when he finally brought them to it. This repeated hardness of heart culminated in forty years of wandering in the wilderness until the entire generation was dead—except for Joshua and Caleb (see Num. 14:26–38).

The psalmist reflects on this long history of failure and sees a danger in our own hearts. Not only did *they* turn away from God despite his miraculous provision but *we*, too, are always in danger of this. It is not always that we wander because God feels distant. Sometimes our sin is so deceitful that we stray from God when his good presence is clear to us. So, today, the day you read this psalm, do not harden your heart.

The failure of the wilderness generation is held out as a warning. Do not be like them. Do not grumble against the God who shepherds you. The last word of the psalm is no mere description of their failures, however, but God's curse on them: "They shall not enter my rest" (Ps. 95:11). They are banned from the promised land. They are banned from God's good rest.

This curse is left hanging in the air as the psalm ends. And we are left to wonder why. Why let this wrathful oath be the final note sung? Why end a psalm of praise with a declaration of condemnation of God's own people?

Is it possible that this psalm has yet more to say?

Reading Hebrews

Let's observe how the author reads Psalm 95 in Hebrews 3:12–4:11:

> Take care, brothers, lest there be in any of you an evil, unbelieving heart, leading you to fall away from the living God. But exhort one another every day, as long as it is called "today," that none of you may be hardened by the deceitfulness of sin. For we have come to share in Christ, if indeed we hold our original confidence firm to the end. As it is said,
>
> > "Today, if you hear his voice,
> > do not harden your hearts as in the rebellion."
>
> For who were those who heard and yet rebelled? Was it not all those who left Egypt led by Moses? And with whom was he provoked for forty years? Was it not with those who sinned, whose bodies fell in the wilderness? And to whom did he swear that they would not enter his rest, but to those who were disobedient? So we see that they were unable to enter because of unbelief.
>
> Therefore, while the promise of entering his rest still stands, let us fear lest any of you should seem to have failed to reach it.

For good news came to us just as to them, but the message they heard did not benefit them, because they were not united by faith with those who listened. For we who have believed enter that rest, as he has said,

> "As I swore in my wrath,
> 'They shall not enter my rest,'"

although his works were finished from the foundation of the world. For he has somewhere spoken of the seventh day in this way: "And God rested on the seventh day from all his works." And again in this passage he said,

> "They shall not enter my rest."

Since therefore it remains for some to enter it, and those who formerly received the good news failed to enter because of disobedience, again he appoints a certain day, "Today," saying through David so long afterward, in the words already quoted,

> "Today, if you hear his voice,
> do not harden your hearts."

For if Joshua had given them rest, God would not have spoken of another day later on. So then, there remains a Sabbath rest for the people of God, for whoever has entered God's rest has also rested from his works as God did from his.

Let us therefore strive to enter that rest, so that no one may fall by the same sort of disobedience. (Heb. 3:12–4:11)

Hebrews 3:7–4:11 is an extended meditation on the second half of Psalm 95. The author picks up the psalm's call not to harden hearts as the wilderness generation did, warning his readers of the danger of an unbelieving heart and a life of disobedience. Through a series of questions, the author recounts the story of the wilderness generation and their unwillingness to follow the voice of God. Through unbelief and disobedience, they earned God's wrath and perished in the wilderness. Through their hard, unbelieving hearts, they were deceived by sin and thought that the good promises of God were worse than the offerings of slavery in Egypt. They stand as a warning to us, and we should not follow their example.

Fairly straightforward. Yet Hebrews has more to say about this psalm. Although the negative example is important, the author's next interpretive move is even more significant. As the argument transitions into Hebrews 4, the author makes a surprising claim, "Therefore, while the promise of entering his rest still stands, let us fear lest any of you should seem to have failed to reach it" (Heb. 4:1).

Did you catch that?

The psalm ends in a curse: "They shall not enter my rest." Hebrews sees a promise: some will enter God's rest. Throughout Hebrews 4, the author argues that everything denied to the wilderness generation (and later, everything left unfinished by the conquest generation under Joshua) is now offered to the church through Christ. How does he do this? How does he read a blessing for us in the contours of a curse for them?

Under the inspiration of the Spirit, the author to the Hebrews is a careful interpreter of Scripture. He knows that Psalm 95 is a *psalm*, an inspired song of praise meant for God's people throughout history. Because of this, he knows that no detail is wasted, nothing is superfluous.

The author seizes on the word "today." If the psalmist calls us to action today, then there is hope for today. The psalmist, David, spoke hundreds of years after the exodus. The "today" offered is not limited to the people of the exodus but is extended to God's people who hear this psalm. The logic runs from there: if today we can succeed where the wilderness generation failed, then we can be blessed where they were cursed. Their hearts were hardened, and so they were banned from God's rest. If, by God's grace, you do not harden your heart, what will happen? You will be received into God's rest.

The author shows us that this rest was never just the land of Canaan but, rather, is a time of joyful rest and worship in the presence of God—a final Sabbath rest for God's people. The author looks back to God's rest after creation and reveals that it is this enduring peace of God that we are invited to enter. This is no arbitrary move. While the author is drawing a connection between God's rest in Psalm 95:11 and God's rest in Genesis 2:3, he's also following the guidance of the psalmist. Psalm 95 calls us to praise God as Creator in terms taken from Genesis 1. Psalm 95 ends in a curse on the wilderness generation that they would not enter God's rest. But which rest could that be? The rest discussed in that same creation account in Genesis. We move from a description of the third day to that of the seventh day. God entered into rest and welcomes all his people into it. The end restores and builds on the beginning.

God rested from all his works on the seventh day, and as we draw near to God we are welcomed into this lasting and abiding rest. In the presence of God we will find an end to all our striving, an end to all frantic and burdened work. But do not misunderstand; this rest is not mere inactivity but a Sabbath rest. It is a time of worship but also of feasting, fellowship, and joy. The rest that God welcomes us into is a rest of eternal celebration among all God's people.

And how now shall we enter it? Just like the generation of the conquest, we need a leader to go before us. The author tells us, "For if Joshua had given them rest, God would not have spoken of another day later on" (Heb. 4:8). To appreciate the full effect of what Hebrews is saying, you need to know just a little Greek. In Greek (and Hebrew) "Joshua" and "Jesus" are the same name. We translate them differently for historical reasons, but they are the same name. If you were to read the letter to the Hebrews in its original Greek language, then, you would be struck by the statement, "If Jesus had given them rest."

This gives the game away. There was a lesser "Jesus," a forerunner for the people who led them into the land of promise. Although none of God's good words to him failed, the people did not ultimately enter rest. There has now come another, greater Jesus who has gone into God's presence as our forerunner and as the anchor of our hope, who sits in the heavenly Jerusalem and guarantees that where he is, we will be also.

How do we enter this rest? We follow our leader Jesus into the presence of God.

Reading Psalm 95 Again

Psalm 95 meets us today. As in Genesis, creation is followed by fall. God made the world, rested from his works, and enjoyed fellowship with man, but then man fell away from God. In Psalm 95, we are called to praise God the Creator who shepherds his people. He not only created us from dust but also by his grand acts of deliverance made us a people for his own possession, led and fed by his own hand.

And yet, as his redeemed people, we are reminded of another time when God's people were redeemed and called to worship God their Maker but fell away from him. In the wilderness they tested God, and the rest first introduced in Genesis, the rest declared again in God's redemption of the people from Egypt, was rejected. Because of their unbelief and disobedience, God's wrath broke out against the people and forbade them from entering the promised land—the earthly symbol of God's rest.

Many years later, David composed this psalm in which he speaks of "today." You, today, are called to praise God your Maker. You, today, are called not to harden your heart as did the wilderness generation. And you, today, are called to hear a note of promise as the psalm ends in curse. They did not enter, but you can.

The psalm does not finally end in curse because it is a psalm. It is meant to be sung again and again, and it is meant for today. This is no mere account of past events but a present charge to God's people. This is a song to be sung by God's faithful people who are trained by Scripture to hear the curses of God as negative images of the promise. This is a song that narrates not only a past of judgment but also a today of redemption. The words of a psalm demand a resolution that they do not themselves provide. As the words cease, the song is profoundly unfinished. By heeding the call for "today," we finish the psalm and find the blessing mirrored in the curse.

Conclusion

The threads of Genesis, Exodus, Numbers, and Joshua all weave together and run through Psalm 95. Under the leadership of Jesus, the greater Joshua, you are given a promise of entering God's rest through faith in him, in obedience to his word, and following the path he sets before you. Psalm 95, whenever you sing or read it, is a call to continued faithfulness and worship. It indeed is fitting as a daily song to God because it confronts us every day, so long as it is called "today," with a chance to worship God as King, Creator, shepherd, and Redeemer. As we draw near to God through Christ, we enter rest even as he entered rest, and we find ourselves in the caring presence of God who has prepared all this for us, the sheep of his hand.

Discussion Questions

1. How does the rest of God in Genesis 1 connect to the rest offered to us in Christ?

2. How should we deal with negative examples in the Old Testament?

3. The author of Hebrews finds a blessing in the curse of Psalm 95. Is this method generally applicable?

4. What does it mean to rest in God?

7

Psalm 102

THERE ARE, FUNDAMENTALLY, two different ways to feel small.

The first is to be overwhelmed.

When I was young, I was terrified by the thought of traveling over large bodies of water. It didn't matter whether it was by boat or plane. If I could not see shore on every side, I did not want to go. I could not stop myself from thinking about how enormous the expanse of water was, how you could go down in it without a trace—with no mark of your passage. I was terrified by the sheer quantity of water and my small size compared to it. It did not matter that the boat was big or the airplane was high. They were as insignificant as toys next to all that water. I was overwhelmed.

Some people, I am told, seek out this feeling. In the presence of large waves or towering mountains they wish to feel overwhelmed by the sublime grandeur of height or depth. I do not share this instinct. I do not want to feel small in this way.

The second way to feel small is to be held.

When someone is caring for us, when we are unable to provide for ourselves and they step in to do what we need but cannot accomplish, we feel small. But this is a smallness that welcomes the help of those who carry us. There may be pain in our inability, but there is a comfort when that inability is met by the loving ability of another. My children are small, and they do not perceive themselves to be bigger when I scoop them up and hold them. But they are glad that arms bigger than their own can lift them up. They feel small, and they feel safe.

Psalm 102 is a psalm of someone who is brought low by suffering. The psalmist's sins, afflictions, and enemies conspire together to reduce him to the dust. His smallness is put on full display, and in it he calls out to the God who holds him in everlasting arms, and he is made safe.

Reading Psalm 102

The superscription of Psalm 102 sets us in the moment of suffering: "A Prayer of one afflicted, when he is faint and pours out his complaint before the Lord." This is not some calm reflection after the storm has passed but rather a cry from the whirlwind. This is particularly helpful for us because it models a prayer from a place, not of safety, but of certainty. God will deliver us. Many psalms present us with a retrospective. We see the praise given to God for past deliverance. But when we suffer, when living makes us faint and burns us to ash, we do not have the benefit of retrospect. We need to live through it. In this psalm, we see how. A way is provided for us as we pour out our complaint before the Lord along with the psalmist.

Cry for Deliverance (Ps. 102:1–2)

> Hear my prayer, O Lord;
>   let my cry come to you!

> Do not hide your face from me
>   in the day of my distress!
> Incline your ear to me;
>   answer me speedily in the day when I call! (Ps. 102:1–2)

In his suffering, the psalmist cries out to God. This may seem obvious. It may be the kind of thing you are inclined to skip over. But note that he does not wait for his suffering to end before speaking to God. He does not delay until he is free from sin or has a handle on the situation before asking God to be near and answer him speedily. The presence of distress is enough reason to call on the Lord to deliver. The moment we feel as if God's good presence has been denied us, we have enough reason to call on him not to hide his face.

In this opening, we are given little context. That will come later. It is enough that the psalmist suffers, that he is in the day of his distress. His cry centers on a desire that God would hear and be present. He longs for an answer, presumably the alleviation of his suffering, and he knows that the answer will come with the blessing of the face of the Lord.

A Small Sufferer and a Big God (Ps. 102:3–17)

> For my days pass away like smoke,
>   and my bones burn like a furnace.
> My heart is struck down like grass and has withered;
>   I forget to eat my bread.
> Because of my loud groaning
>   my bones cling to my flesh.
> I am like a desert owl of the wilderness,
>   like an owl of the waste places;

I lie awake;
>   I am like a lonely sparrow on the housetop.
> All the day my enemies taunt me;
>   those who deride me use my name for a curse.
> For I eat ashes like bread
>   and mingle tears with my drink,
> because of your indignation and anger;
>   for you have taken me up and thrown me down.
> My days are like an evening shadow;
>   I wither away like grass.
>
> But you, O Lord, are enthroned forever;
>   you are remembered throughout all generations.
> You will arise and have pity on Zion;
>   it is the time to favor her;
>   the appointed time has come.
> For your servants hold her stones dear
>   and have pity on her dust.
> Nations will fear the name of the Lord,
>   and all the kings of the earth will fear your glory.
> For the Lord builds up Zion;
>   he appears in his glory;
> he regards the prayer of the destitute
>   and does not despise their prayer. (Ps. 102:3–17)

The psalmist describes his suffering. His distress is deep. There seems to be no aspect of life that it does not reach. His pain is physical and emotional, in his heart and in his bones. His alienation is social and spiritual. He is separated from friends and surrounded by enemies. Yet this is not the righteous sufferer of other psalms.

He is not persecuted for his allegiance to the Lord, but rather in his suffering he sees the anger of God. He has done wrong.

This is not to say that suffering is necessarily the result of sin or that, because we have acted wrongly, we deserve that others should act wrongly toward us. In this instance, the psalmist does see some link between the ways in which he has sinned and his current experience of suffering, but we are not to generalize this point. Rather, this psalm shows that the psalmist's cry to God as deliverer is based on something other than himself. The plea for God to answer quickly is founded on who God is rather than on how well the psalmist has lived. He looks forward to the time that God will turn his face toward him with blessing—not because he has never merited the anger of God but rather in the full knowledge of his own sin.

The psalmist paints his condition through the repetition of three images: grass, bread, and birds.[1] His heart, his very self, withers like grass (102:4, 11). Grass throughout Scripture is an image of impermanence, the quickly fading stuff of this world that is here today and gone tomorrow. Because of his suffering, the psalmist feels as if he has already withered away. His short life has come to an end, and he is but a husk of what he once was.

He forgets to eat his bread (102:4), and instead he eats ashes as his bread (102:9). Because of his suffering, he cannot bring himself to eat. It could be because of intense depression over his

---

[1] The psalmist further draws our attention to this through a literary device called a *chiasm*, where repetition of words or themes is used to form the structure of a unit. The structure can be thought of as something like ABC C'B'A'. References to grass form the outside in 102:4 (A) and 102:11 (A'). Then references to bread form a layer in 102:4 (B) and 102:9 (B'). Finally, references to birds form the innermost layer in 102:6 (C) and 102:7 (C'). Sometimes, the inner layer should be seen as central or most emphatic, but that is not clearly the case here.

circumstances, great anxiety over his fate, or deep sorrow over his sin, but he cannot bring himself to eat. Eating ash for bread—that is, for his food—is itself an image of suffering and possibly of repentance. He turns away from food that would strengthen him but instead spends his time chewing on his own sorrow and suffering. As we sing with him, we are reminded of times when we have been too depressed to get out of bed, too anxious to eat, too consumed with our guilt or our pain to think of anything other than what we hate.

He is like a "desert owl of the wilderness" (102:6), "an owl of the waste places" (102:6), or "a lonely sparrow on the housetop" (102:7). He is small and alone. The emphasis in all these images is isolation. People do not go to the wilderness and the waste places. Sparrows are social birds, often found in large groups, but the psalmist finds himself alone, bereft of his friends and companions. Indeed, the only other people to be found are his enemies (102:8). There may be some further significance in the use of the birds translated as "desert owl" and "owl." These are unclean birds that live in places of death—in desolate ruins (Isa. 34:11; Zeph. 2:14). He is unclean and alone, far from any who could do him good. Where once there was life, there is only wreck and desolation.

"But you, O Lord, are enthroned forever" (Ps 102:12). The psalmist moves from his small, fleeting life to the eternal stability of God Almighty. This is no non sequitur; this is not some unrelated theological statement meant to distract from the psalmist's suffering. It is precisely in the eternal, unchanging reign of the Lord that we can find our hope. Because he rules, because he will never be off his throne, we know that he will act to save.

The psalmist is certain:

> You will arise and have pity on Zion;
>   it is the time to favor her;
>   the appointed time has come. (102:13)

There is no doubt now in the psalmist's mind. God will act to deliver his people. In this verse, the scope of the psalm widens. We find that not only does the psalmist suffer but so too do the other servants of God (102:14). Zion, the city of God, has been downtrodden and needs God to build her up (102:16). The city of God is filled with the destitute who need the pity of the Lord (102:13, 17). This could historically situate the psalm after the exile or when Jerusalem was surrounded by armies but not yet overcome. Regardless, we find the fate of the psalmist tied up with the fate of the people of God. God will show mercy to this sufferer, even as he shows mercy to Zion.

The smallness and sinfulness of the suffering psalmist do nothing to shake his certainty. It may be that he has withered as the grass. It may be that Zion has been reduced to rubble and dust. He may flit among the ruins surrounded by enemies. Even so, the eternally reigning God will act. Now is the time. He hears the prayer (102:17). Precisely in the bigness of God do God's people find their security. We may be made small by our suffering, yet God does not despise the prayer of the lowly (102:17). His glory and power stoop to save the small sinner and sufferer who calls on him.

Declaration of Deliverance (Ps. 102:18–22)

> Let this be recorded for a generation to come,
>   so that a people yet to be created may praise the LORD:
> that he looked down from his holy height;
>   from heaven the LORD looked at the earth,

> to hear the groans of the prisoners,
>> to set free those who were doomed to die,
> that they may declare in Zion the name of the Lord,
>> and in Jerusalem his praise,
> when peoples gather together,
>> and kingdoms, to worship the Lord. (Ps. 102:18–22)

The psalmist now speaks from the perspective of God's delivered people. It may be, as the next portion of the psalm suggests, that he says this prophetically in certain anticipation. Regardless, as we sing with him we can declare it with equal certainty for all his past acts of deliverance and all his wondrous works to come.

God's acts of salvation are to be recorded for all posterity. Even nations not yet formed must know what God has done. The stories of his acts of deliverance go before us, meeting us with a declaration of who God is and what he has done as we enter the world.

What did God do and why did he do it? Continuing the language of the small and the large, the psalmist tells us,

> He looked down from his holy height;
>> from heaven the Lord looked at the earth. (102:19)

The distance between God's heights and our lowliness is emphasized to make it even more significant that he has acted to save us. In this passage we have something like an inverse Babel. At Babel, mankind thought it could make itself great enough to ascend to heaven, and from his great height the Lord "came down" to see the project (Gen. 11:5) and then again went down to them in judgment (11:7). The greatness of man's self-made glory is so small that the Lord must come down, so to speak, even to see it.

But in Psalm 102, in the moment of our smallness and suffering, God sees us from the heights of heaven. God hears the groans of the prisoners and saves those doomed to die (Ps. 102:20). No sigh is so small that it does not fill the halls of heaven. Like the father who saw his returning son from a long way off (Luke 15:20), God Almighty, enthroned forever, is ever watching for the prayer of his suffering people.

And why did God do it? That his name might be known in Zion by all nations. As throughout Scripture, God makes his glory and his name known through his acts of salvation. The point of an act of deliverance is never the mere alleviation of suffering but always so that the person saved is brought into the good presence of the Lord. It is no different in Psalm 102. God saves his people so that they can live with him in the joy of that salvation. But there is one detail that may have skipped your notice on first reading.

Although the declaration of God's name and praise will happen "in Zion" and "in Jerusalem" (Ps. 102:21), who will be offering the worship? It will be "peoples" gathered together and "kingdoms" in Zion "to worship the Lord" (102:22). The saving work that God has done in Zion will cause *other* nations to gather as one with the people of God to offer praise and worship to the Lord, the God of Zion. We might be tempted to ask how this could be. What kind of saving act would bring the kingdoms of the earth to worship the Lord in Jerusalem? But the psalm has no answer for us. Instead, the psalm continues, and the psalmist's suffering reasserts itself.

A Small Sufferer and a Big God Again (Ps. 102:23–28)

> He has broken my strength in midcourse;
>   he has shortened my days.

> "O my God," I say, "take me not away
>   in the midst of my days—
> you whose years endure
>   throughout all generations!"
>
> Of old you laid the foundation of the earth,
>   and the heavens are the work of your hands.
> They will perish, but you will remain;
>   they will all wear out like a garment.
> You will change them like a robe, and they will pass away,
>   but you are the same, and your years have no end.
> The children of your servants shall dwell secure;
>   their offspring shall be established before you.
>   (Ps. 102:23–28)

As the pain of the psalmist breaks into the psalm once more, his hope rises to meet it. As he faces the truth that his suffering comes from God's sovereign hand, he feels his imminent death and attributes it to God. Yet in the same breath he cries out to God for deliverance. The discipline of the Lord may yet relent, and the psalmist may be restored. Even as we feel the hand of the Lord heavy on us in discipline, that same hand may establish us securely. God does not work without purpose and will not afflict one moment more than is necessary for his plans for us.

The psalmist cannot think of the looming shortness of his days without thought of the enduring years of the Lord. Short-lived humanity, withered grass that we are, by our very ephemerality calls to mind the eternal stability of God. And again, this is not some free association meant to distract the psalmist from his present problems. Yes, the premature end of his life haunts him, but if hope is to be found, it is in the unending and unchanging life of God.

Even if the psalmist lived a good long life, he would one day die. The rocks of the earth would stand, and the stars of the heavens would wheel above as if he had never lived. Yet even these endure but the span of a breath compared to God. He made them, so he was there before them. He will change them like a robe, and he will remain after he does so. The world wears out through its long years of use. At the end of it all, God will not be one bit older, for age and time have no meaning for him.

The unchanging, never-ending God is our hope. Because he does not change, his past acts of salvation for his people tell us that he will always act to save them. Because he has no end, neither will his promises end.

He has acted decisively in salvation for his people. Therefore, the nations will praise God in Zion. And yet there is more that God will do. He will yet renew the heavens and the earth. And even through this, even as all things will be changed,

> The children of [his] servants shall dwell secure;
>   their offspring shall be established before [him]. (102:28)

His eternal stability is our hope, because he will give it to us. His people are unshakably secure because he is eternally the same. His eternal stability is our security forever.

Reading Hebrews

> Of the angels he says,
>
> > "He makes his angels winds,
> >   and his ministers a flame of fire."

CHAPTER 7

But of the Son he says,

. . . .

"You, Lord, laid the foundation of the earth in the beginning,
  and the heavens are the work of your hands;
they will perish, but you remain;
  they will all wear out like a garment,
like a robe you will roll them up,
  like a garment they will be changed.
But you are the same,
  and your years will have no end." (Heb. 1:7–8a, 10–12)

We have been here before. This is the continuation of the comparison in Hebrews 1 between Jesus and the angels where, time and time again, Jesus is shown to be superior. Earlier in this book (chap. 5), we looked at the author's use of Psalm 45 to talk about Jesus's eternal throne as exalted King in contrast with the angels' changeability. The author to the Hebrews now continues that same comparison and adds the testimony of Psalm 102, further developing the theme of the eternal stability of the Son of God. Intriguingly, the author does not use the portion of Psalm 102 that is closest to the wording of Psalm 45[2] but instead tells us more, showing us that the Son is not only the eternally unchanging God but also the one who creates and recreates the heavens and the earth.

But what could lead the author of Hebrews to read the psalm in this way? Why take these things that the psalmist attributes to God

---

2 Ps. 102:12: "But you, O Lord, are enthroned forever." Ps. 45:6: "Your throne, O God, is forever and ever."

and make them specifically about the *Son*? Furthermore, in what way are they true about the Son? Do they speak, as does Psalm 45, about the exalted, incarnate Son of God? Or are they true of him in respect to his divinity, things that could be said about the Son equally before the incarnation as after?

There are two separate threads that the author might have followed to reach this conclusion: the intra-psalter thread and the gospel-story thread.

By intra-psalter, I mean that there are clues in the other psalms that we know the author was thinking of as he wrote Hebrews. The first clue, and the one we have already seen, is in Psalm 45. We know that Psalm 45 was on the author's mind as he cited Psalm 102 because he quoted Psalm 45 in the previous verse. It is possible that since both Psalm 45 and Psalm 102 mention an eternal throne or enthronement, the author could have been led to read the two together. Furthermore, from Psalm 22, which the author cites in Hebrews 2, we saw how an act of deliverance performed by and for the Son of God would cause the nations to worship the Lord (Ps. 22:27), precisely in a context that acknowledges the Lord as King over the nations (22:28). All this could have led the author to see how something said of the eternally unchanging and reigning God who performs an act of deliverance that causes the nations to worship the Lord is applicable to the Son of God in particular.

Related to this is the gospel-story thread. We have already seen how the author to the Hebrews reads the Psalms through the lens of the preexistence, incarnation, life, death, resurrection, and ascension of Jesus, the Son of God. When Psalm 102 tells the story of God who looks down from heaven, works salvation in Jerusalem for his suffering people, and will bring all the nations together in Zion in security after the heavens and earth are transformed, it is hard not to read in this the story of Jesus. The Son of God, who has always been God, who created all things and who will remake all things, is also the one who came down to earth to redeem his people.

These threads and this citation of Psalm 102 eventually lead to one of the most surprising declarations of the entire book of Hebrews: "Jesus Christ is the same yesterday and today and forever" (Heb. 13:8). Jesus Christ, who truly took on humanity, lived, died, and rose again, nevertheless remains the unchanging Son of God forever. The infant of Christmas and the sufferer upon the tree of Good Friday ever remains the eternally enthroned and unchanging God.

Hebrews tells us that this portion of Psalm 102 speaks of the Son in his eternal divine glory. If we remember how this citation was introduced (along with that of Psalm 45 discussed in chap. 5), we also learn that God the Father is the one who says this to the Son. In this passage, the Father proclaims to us the Son's true divinity. As God, the Son is coeternal with the Father. God is eternally unchanging and ruling, so the Son, *as God*, is eternally unchanging and ruling. And the Father delights in telling us so.

Reading Psalm 102 Again

Once we see Jesus as the unchanging, ruling, creating, and remaking God of Psalm 102, how does it change our understanding of the whole psalm?

First, it further explains the certainty of the psalmist. How can the psalmist be certain that God will deliver him? How can a sinner who knows his own sin, who feels the discipline and anger of God against his sin, be confident that God will answer his prayer quickly? Because that same God became a man to save him.

Second, it explains the great mystery of the center of the psalm: How will the acts of God in Zion cause the nations and kingdoms of the earth to worship God together? The story of the New Testament charts the path by which all the nations of the earth will come to worship the God of Israel. It will happen through the work of the Son of God who came to save a people from all peoples.

Beyond that, seeing Jesus as the unchanging God on the throne strengthens and deepens the central theological point of Psalm 102: the unchanging rule and character of God are the basis for our certainty of salvation. The God who made all things, the God who remains the same even as the cosmos wears out and is remade anew, the God who sits eternally on the throne over all creation, he is the one who will save his people and who guarantees that every promise he makes will come to fulfillment. He is the one whose stability is our security. It is good for us, eternally good for us, that he does not change.

But the God over the heights of heaven has also come down to us. The bigness of God—his eternal, unchanging power—works salvation for us. He holds us in his power. The infinite greatness of God became small to rescue us. He hears the groan of the prisoner and delivers the one condemned to death because he himself became that prisoner. He himself bore our death in his body on the tree.

The glory of the gospel, the profound mystery of it all, is that the unchanging God, who remains the same, who can never be off the throne, who cannot die, died a human death to rescue us from death. His servants and their children and a people yet to be made shall be eternally secure even as the heavens and the earth give way and are remade because of what he has done.

CHAPTER 7

Conclusion

Your strength may be broken in midcourse. You may wither as the grass or be as desolate as ruins. Your only food may be the ashes of your own guilt and sorrow. Your suffering may reduce you and bring you low. Even so, the eternal God will cause his face to shine on you. Your prayer will be heard, and you will be delivered. Let this be known to all future generations. God from his highest heaven has heard your cry. He hears it still. And he has come down to save you. He has come down with all his unchanging power to rescue you. You will be delivered from death. You will be set free from your prison. He will hear you swiftly. And you will be held securely in his power and presence forever.

Discussion Questions

1. How does it help us that God does not change?

2. What is surprising about this sentence: "Jesus Christ is the same yesterday and today and forever"?

3. How do we pray while we are suffering?

4. What does it mean for God to not hide his face from us?

8

Psalm 110

OVER THE PAST SEVERAL YEARS, I have developed a fondness for murder mystery novels. I am not entirely sure what this may say of me. Perhaps I have an unhealthy preoccupation with death. Perhaps I am approaching middle age. Whatever the cause, it has happened. I enjoy relaxing with a mystery novel and following the road the author paves.

In a way that sometimes frustrates my friends who also enjoy such literary adventures, however, I almost never care about guessing who the culprit is. If the book is well written, I am confident that although enough evidence is given that I could figure out who did it, I also know that it has been presented in a way that my guess is likely to be wrong. This is the true beauty of a mystery. Sure, there may be false trails or red herrings, but in a really well-written mystery, you are not only given the right clues but also given enough of them so that you could piece the mystery together. But here is the catch: without the right framing, without seeing it in exactly the way that the detective sees it in the climactic moments, the evidence seems like a string of disconnected information that does not lead anywhere.

CHAPTER 8

But then, once your frame shifts, once you see things the way the detective sees them, all the clues you could not understand become clear and coherent. Everything tells a single story. In a flash you can see not only the errors of your failed interpretations but also the truth that should have been obvious the whole time. It had always been there, right in front of you. All you needed was to look at it in the right way, and everything becomes clear.

Psalm 110 is a bit of a mystery. It is filled to the brim with suggestive details and hints. There is a king. There are nations. The king is a priest. The "Lord" speaks to David's Lord. Morning dew settles and winter brooks flow. An obscure figure from the past is mentioned but not explained. It is clear that something important is said, but it is not clear on first reading what it means.

Until you read the psalm with the right framing. Then, everything clicks into place.

Somewhat surprisingly, this is the psalm most frequently referred to in the New Testament. Not the calming pastoral care of Psalm 23 that Christians are familiar with. Not the proclamation of the Son in Psalm 2 or the clear crucifixion scene of Psalm 22. No psalm comes close to the frequent and widespread use by New Testament authors that Psalm 110 enjoys. And this was no arbitrary choice. The New Testament authors were not drawing from general understandings of the psalm that existed in their culture but that are lost to us. Rather, Jesus's own teaching in the last week of his earthly ministry taught his followers how to understand this enigmatic psalm. A masterful exegetical detective, Jesus presented the key to understanding this psalm so that it could never be seen differently.

Reading Psalm 110

On our first reading of Psalm 110, we will read in much the same way I read a mystery novel. Before we ask the all-important question—*Who is this?*—we will catalog the ways that David describes this person and his work. Of course, in the back of our minds will linger Jesus's question about how the person described in this psalm can be both David's son and David's Lord (Matt. 22:45). But before jumping to the answer, we will see just how extraordinary this son and Lord of David is.

To do that, we will look at the psalm in three stanzas that show the Lord's repose, the Lord's roles, and the Lord's wrath.

The Lord's Repose (Ps. 110:1)

A Psalm of David.

> The LORD says to my Lord:
>   "Sit at my right hand,
> until I make your enemies your footstool." (Ps. 110:1)

The psalm begins with something that seems like an ending. The characters are already set. The time of tension is over. The "LORD" speaks to "my Lord" and welcomes him to sit at his right hand. Now we wait until the next act begins.

But who are these characters? What story are we entering?

The first person we meet is the author, David, composing this song about a king greater than himself. The second person is the "LORD." The capital letters let you know that in Hebrew we have the divine name. Theologically, as Christians we know that sometimes this is used simply to refer to God without specifying one particular divine person. Other times, the divine name is used of an individual person within the Godhead: the Father, the Son, or the Spirit. Only context tells us which.

The "Lord" speaks. He addresses "my Lord"—that is, David's Lord. This is the normal word one finds in the Old Testament for a lord, a sovereign, one who has authority over another. As David plucks his harp, he overhears a conversation between the Lord God and his Lord. David does not name this individual but only refers to his title, his authority. In the story of the Old Testament, we cannot know who this is, but we are given a hint of his greatness. David was a man after God's own heart, a king specially chosen by God to rule over his people. David was a man of great power and favor with God. He returned the ark to Jerusalem. He reigned over the people of God for forty years. He prepared a way for the building of the temple. He himself received an eternal covenant from God, blessings for himself and his posterity. He was the prophet and king who conquered and sang mightily for God's glory and by God's strength. And yet even he acknowledged the greatness of another. As he heard the Lord God speak to this (as yet unnamed) individual, he knew that he heard an address to his own Lord.

And the words that the Lord God spoke only raise our view of this Lord higher: "Sit at my right hand." There can be no higher invitation. This Lord is called to sit in heaven at the throne of God. This is shocking in at least two ways.

First, to sit at someone's right hand is to share in his power or authority in such a way as to have either an equal or a similar amount of authority as he does. The following discussion of this psalm and its use in Hebrews will show how this is a statement of equal authority between God and this Lord. But even before that is made clear, this statement is near scandalous. How can someone come so close to God in authority that they sit enthroned at his right hand? To say such a thing of a mere human, even a great one like David, would be blasphemy. So how can it be true of David's Lord?

Second, although the Bible includes few scenes set in heaven, those we encounter seem to establish a pattern. In heaven, God sits and others stand. In the great visions of the prophets, God is seated on a throne (Isa. 6:1; Ezek. 1:26). On a smaller scale, when Micaiah speaks of his vision against Ahab, he says, "I saw the Lord sitting on his throne, and all the host of heaven standing beside him on his right hand and on his left" (1 Kings 22:19). This also seems to be the picture when the sons of God present themselves before the Lord in Job (Job 1:6). When created beings, even high angels, are in the presence of the Lord in heaven, they stand in attendance. He sits enthroned. Yet in Psalm 110, David's Lord is invited to sit at God's right hand. The whole Old Testament seems to draw a line between the one who can sit in heaven—God—and those who must stand—everyone else. Somehow, though, David's Lord gets to sit.

What's more, he gets to sit and wait as God works for him. This Lord will put all of his enemies under his feet. He shall conquer, but it is God who will conquer for him. David's Lord will sit at the right hand of God waiting for a future day when God subdues his enemies for him.

The Lord's Roles (Ps. 110:2–4)

> The Lord sends forth from Zion
>   your mighty scepter.
>   Rule in the midst of your enemies!

CHAPTER 8

> Your people will offer themselves freely
> > on the day of your power,
> > in holy garments;
> from the womb of the morning,
> > the dew of your youth will be yours.
> The LORD has sworn
> > and will not change his mind,
> "You are a priest forever
> > after the order of Melchizedek." (Ps. 110:2–4)

The middle verse of this stanza (110:3) is possibly the hardest verse to understand in this entire book. Because of that, we are going to skip it—not entirely but for the moment. By looking at 110:2 and 110:4, we will learn more about who David's Lord is and what he does. In that context, we will be able to understand a little of the response to him as depicted in 110:3.

The first thing David's Lord does is reign. He has a scepter and is commanded to rule, so he must be some kind of king. Yet, the image of repose from 110:1 continues somewhat. His scepter goes forth but not because he advances it with his armies. Rather, God ("the LORD") sends it forth (110:2). The expansion of his kingdom is God's doing. Divine action establishes this kingdom. However it spreads and wherever he rules, it is not in the normal way of human kingdoms. If anyone is within the bounds of this king's rule, it is because God has spread his reign over him.

Moreover, he rules in the midst of his enemies. His kingdom is embattled on every side. His subjects are surrounded by those who would oppose this kingdom. We already know from 110:1 that this Lord has enemies and that they will ultimately be subdued by God. But now we know that, even before his enemies are finally defeated, his kingdom will expand in the midst of his enemies. Those who set themselves against this king will not win. In the end, they will become his footstool. In the meantime, they will watch his scepter advance and his rule enlarge even in their very midst.

But he is not only a king. In a sudden turn, the psalm informs us that he is also a priest:

The Lord has sworn
  and will not change his mind,
"You are a priest forever
  after the order of Melchizedek." (110:4)

It is hard to imagine a more solemn declaration than this. Rarely in Scripture does God swear oaths. God's word alone is irrevocable. To show the unshakeability of his purposes to those who are prone to waver in their faith, occasionally he speaks in terms of oath or promise. In 110:4, to show the certainty of this divine word, the Lord not only swears an oath but declares that he will not change his mind. This is added not because the Lord is prone to go back on his word; he would never do such a thing. Rather, we are told this because we are so slow to believe. This is a matter of absolute certainty, and the Lord wishes our confidence in it to be as stable as his commitment to it.

And to what has the Lord irrevocably committed himself? To install David's Lord as an eternal priest after the order of Melchizedek. This may not be what you would have expected.

The Lord's oaths and covenants tend to have a historical, redemptive reach. In Genesis 22, the Lord swore by himself to Abraham and reaffirmed the covenant to bless all nations on the earth through

Abraham's offspring (Gen. 22:15–19). In 2 Samuel 7, God made a covenant with David, promising a throne and a kingdom that would never end, with God's love ever upon it (2 Sam. 7:4–17). In Psalm 110:4, God swears to an individual—emphatically declaring that this oath will not change—that this person will forever be . . . a priest of an obscure order?

At the least, we can say that this shows us several significant new details about David's Lord. He is immortal; otherwise, he could not be a priest forever. He is both king and priest, a set of offices kept separate under the old covenant. He is also a special kind of priest, a priest like Melchizedek.

Melchizedek is only mentioned in one other story in the Old Testament—when Abram met him and was blessed by him in Genesis 14. Melchizedek, king of Salem (likely what would later become Jerusalem) and priest of "God Most High" (Gen. 14:18), met Abram after he had defeated a coalition of kings and rescued his nephew, Lot. Abram gave Melchizedek a tenth of everything he took from the conquered kings after Melchizedek gave him bread, wine, and a blessing (Gen. 14:17–20). Melchizedek also seems to have taught Abram a thing or two about God, because after Abram was blessed by Melchizedek in the name of "God Most High, / Possessor of heaven and earth" (Gen. 14:19), Abram himself swore to the king of Sodom by that same name (14:22).

The scene receives no commentary in Genesis, and we are told nothing about this Melchizedek. We do not know how he became a priest and a king. We do not know how this man who (presumably) was not from Abram's family came to know the true God and worship him. We do not know whether his presentation of bread and wine was an intentionally prophetic act that foretold of God's later provision of bread and wine for his people (cf. Luke 22:17–20;

John 6:53–58). Almost any question we can ask about Melchizedek ends in the same answer: we do not know![1]

But we do know that he was a priest. And he was not a priest in the same way that Aaron and his sons were priests. Melchizedek did not operate under the Mosaic covenant that legislated the Aaronic priesthood, because he lived before it was established. We do not know exactly what Melchizedek's priesthood was like, but we know it was different from that of Aaron and his sons.

David's Lord, then, will forever be a priest. His priesthood will be different from the Aaronic kind; it will be like that of Melchizedek, the king and priest who lived before him and blessed God's people in the person of Abram.

Now let's return to Psalm 110:3:

> Your people will offer themselves freely
> > on the day of your power,
> > in holy garments.

This priest-king will not merely sit back in repose. The day of his power is coming. As the psalm goes on to show, his enemies will not forever be allowed to rage against him. His might will be put on display. It will be a day not only for the destruction of his enemies, however, but also for the glory of his people. They will gladly advance with him in holy array. His power will be their splendor. His might will overflow in the midst of their holiness. They will gladly join him as he goes forth.

Then comes the really tricky part of 110:3:

---

[1] As someone who has studied Hebrews for years, I am most often asked these two questions: "Who wrote Hebrews?" and "Who was Melchizedek?" Unfortunately, after so many years, my answer to both questions remains the same: I have no idea.

> From the womb of the morning,
>> the dew of your youth will be yours.

This declaration may be similar to the first half of the verse. On this day of the Lord's power, from early in the morning, the members of his army—here described as youths—will settle around him like the dew on the grass. Thus, it could be an image of the abundance of his people gathered about him in strength. Most Christian interpretations of this verse throughout history, however, have been influenced by its translation into Greek (the translation that the author of Hebrews most likely would have read), which says, "From the womb, before the morning star I begat you."[2] If this is what it means, then it is a statement of the *sonship* of this king—that is, it could be saying that David's Lord, who is king and priest, is also the Son of God. Psalm 110 and Psalm 2 might be profiles of the same person.

The Lord's Wrath (Ps. 110:5–7)

> The Lord is at your right hand;
>> he will shatter kings on the day of his wrath.
>
> He will execute judgment among the nations,
>> filling them with corpses;
>
> he will shatter chiefs
>> over the wide earth.
>
> He will drink from the brook by the way;
>> therefore he will lift up his head. (Ps. 110:5–7)

The day of power will also be the day of wrath. In stark terms, the judgment of the earth is set before us. The connections to

---

[2] This is my own translation, and "begat" was chosen to show the similarity to Ps. 2:7.

Psalm 2 continue. Although the word translated "shatter" in 110:5 and 110:6 is not the same as the words used in 2:9 ("break"; "dash"), they are synonyms. Kings and chiefs will be shattered. With God's help, nations and kingdoms over the wide earth will be overthrown. David's Lord will be victorious throughout the world, crushing all those opposed to him. His victory will be total and divinely empowered. There will be no refuge against him. In the day of his wrath, nothing opposed to him can stand.

And he himself will be unscathed. He will drink and refresh himself. He will lift up his head in peace. The exact meaning of the final verse of Psalm 110 is obscure, but the direction in which it gestures is clear enough. He will not be wearied or overcome. In his path, as he goes forward, his strength will be renewed, and his head lifted high. He will stand tall in victory, unbowed, unbroken.

Reading Hebrews

It is difficult to summarize the use of Psalm 110 in Hebrews. Whole books have been written on the ways in which the author weaves the themes of Psalm 110 into his own argument. Psalm 110:1 and 110:4 keep reappearing throughout Hebrews in direct citations, allusions, and the bedrock assumptions of the epistle. Hebrews is about the divine Son who became king and priest, seated at God's right hand. In many ways, Hebrews is about the prophecies of Psalm 110 taking place within history.

It is tempting to allow this chapter to take over the rest of the book, expanding and explaining all the ways in which Psalm 110 shows up in Hebrews. Instead of doing that, I will try a more modest approach. Briefly (and *briefly* really is the key word), we will look at the ways in which Hebrews uses Psalm 110 to talk about Jesus,

CHAPTER 8

first as enthroned king and then as priest. After this all-too-short survey, we will return to Psalm 110 to see how the rest of it speaks about Jesus. When we do so, I will revisit some themes from earlier in this book (Jesus the Son who is king over the nations; the Father who speaks to the Son) and I will address the difficult topic that may have caused some unease: David's Lord (Jesus himself!) filling the nations of the earth with corpses.

The Enthronement of the Son

The first sentence of Hebrews sets the agenda for the rest of the epistle. In Greek, Hebrews 1:1–4 is a single, winding sentence that sets out the nature of the Son, his acts, and his superiority over the angels. After the Son is first mentioned in Hebrews 1:2, several relative clauses build on one another to tell us about him. First, the author tells us that the Father appointed the Son heir of everything and that the Father made all things through the Son (1:2). Then he tells us who the Son is—the radiance of God's glory and the imprint of his nature—and what the Son does and has done, how he sustains the universe the Father made through him and how he has made purification for sins (1:3–4). This last section is written in a way that delays a main verb, heaping description on description and anticipating something yet to come. That main verb finally comes when the author tells us that "he sat down at the right hand of the Majesty on high" (Heb. 1:3), a clear allusion to Psalm 110:1.

The author uses this introduction to launch into the chain of citations we have seen several times before, demonstrating Jesus's superiority over the angels. The final flourish in the author's argument in Hebrews 1 is to make the implicit explicit, ending with the epistle's first direct citation of Psalm 110:

And to which of the angels has he ever said,

> "Sit at my right hand
> until I make your enemies a footstool for your feet"?
> (Heb. 1:13)

The author begins and ends his argument about Jesus's superiority to the angels with references to Psalm 110:1. Throughout the epistle, he continues to use the words of Psalm 110 to show us who Jesus is and the exalted position he now holds in heaven (Heb. 8:1; 10:12–13; 12:2). This is no small thing.

Usually, when we speak or think about Jesus, our focus is on what he has done or what he will do. We talk about the cross and the empty grave. We talk about his coming again to bring us home. But we do not talk nearly enough about what Jesus *is* doing. While Hebrews has plenty to say about what Jesus has done (he has made purification for our sins!) and what he will do (he will come again to gather his eagerly awaiting people!), the author also meditates on what Jesus is doing for us now. He presently helps. He presently intercedes. He is currently in the presence of the Father as our anchor and hope. And he does all this because the words of Psalm 110:1 were spoken to him. He has sat down, enthroned at the right hand of God. The argument of Hebrews comes back to this again and again, because we need Jesus to be seated on the throne of heaven. In particular, we need the exalted God-man to be on the throne, redeeming our humanity, guaranteeing our future, representing us to the Father, and ruling over his people. This is not some throwaway verse. It is not significant merely because it tells us that David's son is also David's Lord. Psalm 110:1 tells us where our Lord is and the great power and authority with which he governs all things for us. He is seated at God's right hand.

The Priesthood of the Son

Jesus is seated at God's right hand not only as king but also as priest. While Psalm 110:1 is the single most quoted and alluded to Old Testament passage in the whole New Testament, Hebrews makes even more use of 110:4. Central to the argument of Hebrews is that Jesus is a priest. Just as he really and bodily ascended into heaven and sat at the right hand of God (Ps. 110:1), he also really and bodily is a priest forever after the order of Melchizedek (110:4). Six times the author to the Hebrews revisits Psalm 110:4 (Heb. 5:6, 10; 6:20; 7:11, 17, 21). He explains what it means to be this kind of priest. Jesus's priesthood is not defined by genealogical descent from Levi but rather by the oath of God and an indestructible life (Heb. 7:16, 21). Jesus offered a sacrifice of his own perfect blood to God (Heb. 9:12), and this sacrifice—unlike all the others—fully perfects those who receive it (9:6–14) and, thus, never needs to be repeated (10:1–10).

In Jesus, perfect priest and perfect sacrifice are united, perfectly purifying the people of God. His once-for-all offering of himself has sanctified us forever, setting us apart for the joyful worship and service of God in the world to come. He has made a way for us to draw near to God, and as priest he has sat down on the throne.

Earlier, we saw how sitting in heaven is unusual, a prerogative of God and God alone. While Hebrews does not explicitly comment on this, the author does build on another implication of Jesus's session (the technical term for his sitting on the throne): Priests do not sit. Throughout Leviticus, Numbers, and Deuteronomy, we never find a time when the priests sit during their service. They must always stand. As long as there is work to do, as long as there is a sacrifice to offer or a prayer to be said, they stand. But Jesus sits.

The author makes this comparison and uses it to show that Jesus's sanctifying work is finished. They stand, but he sits. Why? Because his work is done:

> And every priest stands daily at his service, offering repeatedly the same sacrifices, which can never take away sins. But when Christ had offered for all time a single sacrifice for sins, he sat down at the right hand of God, waiting from that time until his enemies should be made a footstool for his feet. For by a single offering he has perfected for all time those who are being sanctified. (Heb. 10:11–14)

See how the priestly role of Psalm 110:4 is mixed with the royal enthronement of 110:1. Jesus sits as king and priest. He is the king who intercedes for his people and represents them to God. He is the priest who sits enthroned at God's right hand. He is both. We need him to be both. Sin made us far from God, unclean, and alienated from his good pleasure and kingdom. Jesus makes us pure. Jesus sets us apart. Jesus enables us to draw near to God. Jesus makes us citizens and sons. He accomplishes it all. He rescues us entirely. And he does it as the enthroned priest-king at the right hand of God, who holds an eternal priesthood and an eternal throne. He will never fail, lose us, or leave our sin undealt with. He cannot. He would not.

Reading Psalm 110 Again

Obviously, Psalm 110 is about Jesus. Jesus is David's Lord. He is the king and priest who sits at the right hand of God. Even in Jesus's physical absence, his kingdom expands, and his scepter advances because God acts on his behalf.

Within the context of the Old Testament, Psalm 110 may indeed be obscure. It contains exalted descriptions of a man greater than any other, greater than any could be in the Old Testament. But once we know the story of the Son of God who became a man, who sat down at the right hand of God until his enemies are made his footstool, our perspective shifts and Psalm 110 falls into focus. We had the pieces all along; we simply did not know how to read them rightly until Jesus came.

But two parts of the psalm still need to be explained in more detail: his kingdom and his wrath.

> The LORD sends forth from Zion
>   your mighty scepter.
>   Rule in the midst of your enemies! (Ps. 110:2)

Where does Jesus now rule? As Christians, regardless of where we fall in the various camps of eschatological views, we can agree on a few things. Jesus is now King. The way Jesus rules now is different from how he will rule after his return. Christians can disagree on how Jesus expresses his rule now or what role we play in Christ's present reign, but we can at least agree that Jesus now reigns and that his reign is not yet what it will be.

Psalm 110:2 shows the spread of his reign in the present age. The final absolute rule will come in the day of his power, the day of his wrath. But right now, his scepter goes forth—that is to say, day by day more people enter his kingdom as its citizens. God is now working to bring more and more people under the good and benevolent rule of Jesus the King. Day by day the good news of his victory spreads, and those who were in the domain of darkness enter into the kingdom of the beloved Son (Col. 1:13). And his scepter advances from Zion. This is nothing more than the pattern we see in the book of Acts, where the gospel goes forth "in Jerusalem and in all Judea and Samaria, and to the end of the earth" (Acts 1:8). The gospel begins in Jerusalem, the city where Jesus died, was raised, and sent the Spirit to his apostles. From there, it will spread to the far reaches of the earth.

And this kingdom spreads in the midst of its enemies. He rules among them. In nations that once did not know Jesus, there are hosts of his followers. In contexts today where people are hostile to Jesus and his kingdom, he claims some as his own and brings them under his rule. No human opposition or demonic enmity can hold back the spread of his kingdom. He rules today in the midst of his enemies by ruling over his people, the church, those who were once his enemies but are now his beloved. As long as it is called today, until the day of his wrath and power comes, he rescues those opposed to him and brings them to himself.

But what about that day of wrath? What about the final verses of Psalm 110? Are we comfortable reading this about Jesus?

> The Lord is at your right hand;
>   he will shatter kings on the day of his wrath.
> He will execute judgment among the nations,
>   filling them with corpses;
> he will shatter chiefs
>   over the wide earth. (Ps. 110:5–6)

Historically, there has been a spiritualizing way of reading passages like this in the Psalms that takes some of the edge off.

Augustine, for example, regularly reads passages like this as referring to conversion.[3] God's enemies are slain, yes, but they are raised again as his friends. God will bring all his opponents down to death, but he will raise them again as his people. Paul speaks of coming to Christ as dying with him and being raised to life with him (Gal. 2:20). And given what God is currently doing, we can say that this is certainly true. We can pray that God would bring his enemies down to the grave—and raise them up again as his worshipers. New life in Christ is offered to all of Jesus's enemies, but that new life is always first encountered as the command to come and die.

Yet this does not seem to capture what the passage means. Nor is redemption all that Scripture speaks of. A day will come when Jesus returns to rescue his people and to judge his enemies. Psalm 110 is no more severe than the book of Revelation or Jesus's own words in the Gospels. It is a fearful and wicked thing to set oneself up as an enemy of God. It is evil to oppose the kingdom of God. It is even more wicked to be a king, ruler, or one with power who sets himself against God. This is why the passage focuses more on the destruction of kings and chiefs than of commoners. Our God is a consuming fire, and to choose to be outside of his kingdom in this life is, ultimately, to choose to be outside of his kingdom forever. With him is life, and apart from him is no life. Given the choice that Jesus presents to us, we choose either life with him or death apart from him—that is, under his judgment and outside of his goodness. Psalm 110 confronts us with the starkness of that reality.

---

3 Augustine is less immediately helpful in Ps. 110:5–6, however, because the Latin translation he was using was slightly different than what we have: "He will execute judgment among the nations, he will rebuild the ruins." Augustine, *Expositions of the Psalms*, vol. 5 (Ps 99–120), trans. Maria Boulding, ed. Boniface Ramsey (New York: New City Press, 2003), 283. This positive note at the end is used by Augustine, but the pattern is one that he resorts to even when the text of Scripture has no such positive swing.

To study the Scriptures, to hear of Jesus and his message, is not to play games. We deal here with things of eternal weight, of ultimate importance. This psalm encourages us not to forget this.

Conclusion

David spoke of his son, his Lord. In prophetic vision he sang of the Messiah, seated at God's right hand, king and priest forever. He declared the spread of his kingdom and the day of his wrath. Jesus shall turn his enemies into his friends. He will conquer all opposition. He made a single offering for his people and sat down in the splendor of his finished work. He now reigns, and he will reign forever.

Psalm 110 provides us with a glorious picture of the Son of God in all his incarnate glory. He has perfectly saved. He ever lives. He is the king and priest we need. All the wide earth will bow before him. He sits now at God's right hand for us and for our salvation.

Discussion Questions

1. What does it mean for Jesus to be priest and king?

2. What is the significance of Jesus sitting at God's right hand?

3. How do we deal with passages of Scripture that talk about God's wrath?

4. What does it mean for Jesus to rule among his enemies today?

9

Psalm 118

BIG WORDS NEVER get the job done.

Sure, they may be useful for precision or to show that you have read all the right books, but rarely does a big word capture the feeling you want it to, especially for the most important events, the deepest things.

There is an emotionally charged scene in *Macbeth* where he grapples with the guilt of the murder he has just committed, and in a rhetorical flourish, Shakespeare writes,

> Will all great Neptune's ocean wash this blood
> Clean from my hand? No, this my hand will rather
> The multitudinous seas incarnadine,
> Making the green one red.[1]

Note the difference in the third and fourth lines. The third line sounds impressive; the fourth tells you what is happening. The

---

[1] William Shakespeare, *The Tragedy of Macbeth*, ed. G. Blakemore, Riverside Shakespeare (Boston, MA: Houghton Mifflin, 1974), 2.2.57–60 (1320).

third line is about the feel of the language itself; the fourth about the extent of the emotion.

Big words may be needed in small contexts, but they never capture the big things of life. This is true of intense emotional experiences, of things like love and fear and friendship. It is also true of the things of God. We could expend the full limits of human language to describe God in his glory and not get far beyond the simple declaration that God is good.

And he is good. All the time.

And all the time, he is good.

Psalm 118 begins and ends with this simple declaration: he is good. He is good, so we should praise him.

Reading Psalm 118

Because Psalm 118 begins and ends with the goodness of God, it can walk us through the darkness of this life. The psalm strikes a consistent and ringing note of praise. Again and again we are called to give thanks to the Lord, to praise him for his steadfast love and constant help. In the face of suffering, adversaries, or hardship, we are called again and again to give praise to the Lord who helps us and who is always good.

I say "again and again" so much because this psalm is not subtle about what it thinks is important. Repetition repeats. God's goodness and the victory that he brings into the lives of his people are stated and restated. So too are the challenges that surround God's worshipers. This frequent repetition serves for emphasis, but more than that, it sets the atmosphere of the psalm. Life may itself seem long and repetitious. The problems you face one year may come back another year. You may seem to go in circles even as your hardships encircle you on every side. But through it all, at every step, God's goodness and help are there. Beyond that, framing the psalm, at the beginning and end—and at the beginning and end of our lives—we find the goodness of God and his steadfast love that endures forever. So as the psalmist calls us, let us praise him.

Call to Praise (Ps. 118:1–4)

> Oh give thanks to the Lord, for he is good;
> for his steadfast love endures forever!
> Let Israel say,
> "His steadfast love endures forever."
> Let the house of Aaron say,
> "His steadfast love endures forever."
> Let those who fear the Lord say,
> "His steadfast love endures forever." (Ps. 118:1–4)

The psalm begins with the call to give thanks to the Lord, to happily acknowledge all that we have received from his goodness. This is the substance of the Christian life. Thanking the Lord is not merely the saying of words. It is not the rushed and half-begrudging thanks said around a table at Thanksgiving before you can dig into your plate. Rather, it is the glad acknowledgement of everything God has done for you and, even more, all the good things that God is for you. To give thanks to the Lord is to know his goodness and reflect it back to him.

We are called to give thanks for two reasons. He is good, and his steadfast love endures forever.

First, he is good. This simple saying reaches further into the depths of who God is than we can know. He is good. All good things are good because they are a little bit like him, because he allows his goodness to come through them. He is good in himself, and he is good to us. The greatest joy of all eternity will be the exploration of the depths and heights of his goodness. We see his goodness in his acts of salvation. We see his goodness in the delights of this present world. We see his goodness in his love for us. And, through a glass, darkly, we see his goodness in himself. We do not yet know—we will never fully know—just how good the God of all goodness is. But he is good. And he delights to share his goodness with us and to be good to us. The good news of the gospel is that God invites us into his goodness, and we will only ever grow in joy as we walk closer and closer to our good God.

Second, his steadfast love endures forever. "Steadfast love" is an awkward grasp at what the single Hebrew word means. This is God's faithfulness to his people. God's steadfast love is the love by which he does not abandon his own. It is the bedrock of our hope, because it places the certainty of our salvation in God's character, not in our own actions. God is good, and God is faithful. And his faithful love to his people endures forever. All heaven and earth will pass away, but his commitment to his people—to each one of them, including you—will never diminish. He is faithful. He faithfully loves. He faithfully loves you forever.

So give thanks to the Lord!

The psalmist calls all God's people to respond in praise. Israel, the covenant people of God, is summoned. The house of Aaron, those set apart for God's priestly service, is called upon. Those who fear the Lord, all believers everywhere, are called to come. Let all of us say, "His steadfast love endures forever." Let all of us know his unending commitment and love toward us!

The Lord Is My Helper (Ps. 118:5–18)

> Out of my distress I called on the LORD;
>   the LORD answered me and set me free.
> The LORD is on my side; I will not fear.

What can man do to me?
The LORD is on my side as my helper;
   I shall look in triumph on those who hate me.
It is better to take refuge in the LORD
    than to trust in man.
It is better to take refuge in the LORD
    than to trust in princes.

All nations surrounded me;
   in the name of the LORD I cut them off!
They surrounded me, surrounded me on every side;
   in the name of the LORD I cut them off!
They surrounded me like bees;
   they went out like a fire among thorns;
   in the name of the LORD I cut them off!
I was pushed hard, so that I was falling,
   but the LORD helped me.

The LORD is my strength and my song;
   he has become my salvation.
Glad songs of salvation
   are in the tents of the righteous:
"The right hand of the LORD does valiantly,
   the right hand of the LORD exalts,
   the right hand of the LORD does valiantly!"

I shall not die, but I shall live,
   and recount the deeds of the LORD.
The LORD has disciplined me severely,
   but he has not given me over to death. (Ps. 118:5–18)

After the initial call to worship, this psalm follows a path that many other psalms do: I was in distress, I called to the Lord, and the Lord delivered me. What stands out is the way in which the psalmist describes this series of events with frequent repetition. "The Lord is on my side" (Ps. 118:6, 7). "It is better to take refuge in the Lord" (118:8, 9). "[They] surrounded me" (118:10, 11, 12). "In the name of the Lord I cut them off" (118: 10, 11, 12). "The right hand of the Lord does valiantly [or "exalts"]" (118:15, 16).

Repetition is not uncommon in the psalms, but this level of word-for-word similarity from one line to another is remarkable. The psalmist does not want us to lose these truths in the details of his particular situation. What comes through is a single, clear message: God helps his people. No matter how great your troubles and how severely they surround you, if you take refuge in the Lord, you will overcome them because the right hand of the Lord will work for you.

The Lord became the psalmist's "helper" (118:7). The Lord is your helper as well. Of course, having God as your helper does not mean that you will win the lottery or succeed in every business venture. But do not let abuses of this truth keep you from believing that the Lord is your helper. The right hand of the Lord does valiantly for you. Take refuge in the Lord, and you will find better security than in any human power. He will help you. He will protect you. He will raise you up. Do not shrink from singing this psalm.

The House of the Lord (Ps. 118:19–27)

> Open to me the gates of righteousness,
>   that I may enter through them
>   and give thanks to the Lord.
> This is the gate of the Lord;
>   the righteous shall enter through it.

> I thank you that you have answered me
>   and have become my salvation.
> The stone that the builders rejected
>   has become the cornerstone.
> This is the Lord's doing;
>   it is marvelous in our eyes.
> This is the day that the Lord has made;
>   let us rejoice and be glad in it.
>
> Save us, we pray, O Lord!
>   O Lord, we pray, give us success!
>
> Blessed is he who comes in the name of the Lord!
>   We bless you from the house of the Lord.
> The Lord is God,
>   and he has made his light to shine upon us.
> Bind the festal sacrifice with cords,
>   up to the horns of the altar! (Ps. 118:19–27)

The psalmist imagines going up to the temple of God. Having called God's people to give thanks to the Lord, the psalmist enters the place where thanks are most fitting, the house of the Lord.

As we sing with him, we are transported to the gates of the temple, asking for them to be opened so that we can go in—closer to where the name of God dwells—so that we can worship God in his presence. And now, we thank God not only for his goodness but also because he has become our salvation (118:21).

At the mention of salvation, the psalmist's attention shifts. No longer is he narrating his own approach through the gates of the Lord, but his mind goes back to the salvation that God has accomplished:

> The stone that the builders rejected
> 	has become the cornerstone.
> This is the Lord's doing;
> 	it is marvelous in our eyes.
> This is the day that the Lord has made;
> 	let us rejoice and be glad in it. (Ps. 118:22–24)

Somehow, without explanation and against expectation, the salvation accomplished by the Lord involves the surprising elevation of something rejected. God has done something in raising up this cornerstone that is marvelous. The day in which this has happened is set apart as the "day that the Lord has made" (118:24). The psalmist does not explain further, but the sudden elevation of this rejected stone has worked salvation so marvelous that he calls all God's people to rejoice and be glad in it.

This past act of salvation promises future salvation. We can pray to the Lord to save us and to prosper our way because of what he has already done. His raising of this rejected stone has shown that the Lord is for us, and if he was once for us, he always will be, because his steadfast love endures forever.

The final stanza of this section reveals that the rejected and exalted stone is a *person*, the one who comes in the name of the Lord. This person is separate from the "we" who praise him (118:26). That is, he is distinct from the people of God. He is not the psalmist who leads us in singing or the congregation at large. Rather, an individual comes to us in the name of the Lord and is blessed. Through this one, the Lord "has made his light to shine upon us" (118:27).

This section ends with an image that would have been common in the temple—a sacrifice. We find ourselves within the temple courts before the great bronze altar. Here on a festival day, when the people of God were all gathered together, the sacrificial animals were bound and offered to God in the midst of the assembly. While this is a strange image for most of us, that is because of our distance from the biblical imagery. This is an image of joy and glad offering, of feasts and celebration. The offerings at the temple were a physical, concrete way of giving thanks to the Lord because he is good, and this image is one of enjoying the goodness of God's provision.

Call to Praise (Ps. 118:28–29)

> You are my God, and I will give thanks to you;
> you are my God; I will extol you.
> Oh give thanks to the LORD, for he is good;
> for his steadfast love endures forever! (Ps. 118:28–29)

The psalm ends where it began. The Lord is God. He is my God, and he is your God. He is not only your Creator but has also come down to you and bound himself to you by his love. He has made himself your God. So thank him. Praise him. Extol and exalt him.

Give thanks to the Lord, for he is good, for his steadfast love endures forever!

Reading Hebrews

Keep your life free from love of money, and be content with what you have, for he has said, "I will never leave you nor forsake you." So we can confidently say,

> "The Lord is my helper;
> I will not fear;
> what can man do to me?" (Heb. 13:5–6)

CHAPTER 9

Fittingly, for our last chapter, we consider the last explicit citation of Scripture in the epistle to the Hebrews, where the author turns to Psalm 118:6–7 to find encouragement for the future. At this point in the letter, the great message of the superiority of Christ has wound down, and the author concludes with a series of exhortations and commands to his audience. The author is concerned that his audience stay close to Christ, that they not abandon Jesus in the trials of life. But following Christ is not a matter of mere words. To follow Jesus is to live a specific kind of life. In Hebrews 13, the author lays out briefly some of what this life entails.

Following Jesus requires contentment in one's circumstances. One way of describing this is to be free from the love of money. Another way of understanding contentment is to live unafraid. Few people love money for the sake of money. Money is loved for what it can do. Or, more often, money is loved for what it can protect us from. No one wants to live paycheck to paycheck. No one wants to be one car breakdown away from an empty bank account. Money protects.

More truthfully, money *promises* protection. Money provides us with an illusion of security, so a love of money reveals an underlying fear of insecurity. All sorts of terrible things might happen in this life. One way we can try to protect ourselves from this is by accumulating as much money as we can, but ultimately, this is a false hope. Rich people die. Some lose everything before they reach the end of their lives. Some keep their wealth but lose everything that makes life worth living. Fear will again sneak in. Safety will one day be lost.

Instead, the Scriptures direct us to put our trust in God. As Hebrews 13 shows us, this is not a blind trust but rather a response to the promise of God. He has said that he will never leave us. The

Lord has given us the words of the psalms to confess that he is our helper. He has committed himself. He has bound himself to us. He will never leave. He will never stop being your helper. So why fear? What can man do to you? What can come that the Lord is not prepared for? What can come apart from his goodness? What we have is what God our helper has given us, so why should we not be content?

Is this declaration in Hebrews about the Father, or does it refer to Jesus as our helper? While the author does not explicitly say, "This citation is about Jesus," as he does with psalms in Hebrews 1, I believe he wants us to see Jesus as our helper in this way in particular.

First, as the author subsequently reflects on God's goodness to the audience's leaders who have passed away, he remarks, "Jesus Christ is the same yesterday and today and forever" (Heb. 13:8). The logic works this way: God was good to them. You can trust that God will be good to you as well. Why? Because Jesus is the same yesterday and today and forever. That means the God who was good to them and will be good to you *is* this same Jesus. It is Jesus who guided them home. It is Jesus who will help you too.

Second, the author uses related words that mean "help" two other times, and both times Jesus is the helper: "For because he himself has suffered when tempted, he is able to help those who are being tempted" (Heb. 2:18). "Let us then with confidence draw near to the throne of grace, that we may receive mercy and find grace to help in time of need" (4:16). In both cases, Jesus, the God-man and priest, helps us. He helps us in our temptation and in our requests to God. Because Jesus, the Son of God, is the priest who ascended to the heavens and sat down at God's right hand, we particularly find that the throne of God is the throne of grace and help for us. Of course it is—it is where Jesus our helper sits.

CHAPTER 9

The connections between Jesus and Psalm 118 go even deeper. You may have noticed that other New Testament books cite verses of Psalm 118. Jesus uses the psalm to describe his own rejection by the Jewish leaders and God's subsequent exaltation of him. In the Gospels, Jesus confronts the chief priests and Pharisees in Jerusalem shortly before his arrest. After a series of parables, he concludes,

Have you never read in the Scriptures:

"The stone that the builders rejected
   has become the cornerstone;
this was the Lord's doing,
   and it is marvelous in our eyes"? (Matt. 21:42 // Mark 12:10–11 // Luke 20:17, quoting Ps. 118:22–23)

Jesus himself tells us that this part of the psalm is about him.

Jesus is the stone that the builders rejected that has become the cornerstone. He is the one who makes salvation possible. He is the one who was cast out by men, accepted by God, and made the source of salvation for all who come to him.

Later in Matthew, Jesus draws on Psalm 118 again to speak about himself. He laments over the coming fate of Jerusalem, knowing how he will be rejected by the people in that city and declares, "How often would I have gathered your children together as a hen gathers her brood under her wings, and you were not willing! See, your house is left to you desolate. For I tell you, you will not see me again, until you say, 'Blessed is he who comes in the name of the Lord'" (Matt. 23:37–39, quoting Ps. 118:26). Again, Jesus says that he is the Savior of God's people described in Psalm 118. He is the one who comes in the name of the Lord. Interestingly, just as

Psalm 118 separates the rejected and exalted stone from the one who comes in the name of the Lord by a cry for salvation, Jesus makes a distinction between his first coming—when he is rejected and then exalted—and his second coming in the name of the Lord—when the people of Jerusalem will see him again and accept him.

We cannot prove that the author to the Hebrews knew these sayings of Jesus, but there is no reason why he would not have. He speaks of the earthly ministry of Jesus, and as a member of the early church he would have known the stories of Jesus's words and works. If he did know of these sayings, then it makes even more sense why he would have seen Jesus as God the helper from Psalm 118. Jesus's own words taught him to read the psalm this way.

Reading Psalm 118 Again

To sing Psalm 118 today is to sing the story of the Christian life. Beginning and ending the psalm with the goodness of God, we find that Jesus is our helper, our cornerstone, and the one who comes (and will come again) in the name of the Lord.

We come first to a call to praise. What is more fitting for the Christian than to praise God for his goodness? His steadfast love endures forever, and it has been extended to you by pure grace in the giving of his Son. You have been made part of his covenant people, those to whom he is faithful, not by birth or blood but by his undeserved love set on you. You are made not only part of his people but also a priest of God, able to draw near to him without anyone intervening. So you, of all people, should gladly declare, "His steadfast love endures forever!"

And yet this life is beset by troubles. Psalm 118 tells us of Jesus's work for us in our past distress and his promise to us for all future suffering.

CHAPTER 9

> Out of my distress I called on the LORD;
>   the LORD answered me and set me free.
> The LORD is on my side; I will not fear.
>   What can man do to me?
> The LORD is on my side as my helper;
>   I shall look in triumph on those who hate me.
>   (Ps. 118:5–7)

Here is your own story. You once were chained by your sins, but you called to the Lord, and he set you free. In so doing, he proved that he was on your side. Jesus has made himself your helper. He was faithful to save you and make you his. How can he not be faithful to save you again and again? What can man do to you? What can any enemy of your soul do to you? The Lord Jesus is on your side as your helper; you will triumph.

However, this triumph is not the absence of suffering but provision through suffering. Four times the psalmist mentions enemies surrounding him (118:10–12). Again and again, you will feel threatened. Again and again, you will be nearly overwhelmed. The world and the devil will do their best to break you. Your enemies will gather round. But "in the name of the LORD I cut them off!" (118:10, 11, 12). You will overcome. The right hand of the Lord will work valiantly for you (118:15–16). The right hand of the Lord will exalt you (118:16).

For followers of Jesus, this does not mean that hardship will be elminated in this life. But there is a life to come. We believe in the God who raises from the dead. You will overcome every hardship and enemy. You will trample on sin, suffering, and the devil himself. And you will do all this because the Lord will raise you up. When he returns, he will raise you up bodily to a life of joy that never ends and never stumbles. You will overcome, and you will overcome forever. You will be exalted by the help of the Lord in the resurrection. Indeed, you will be able to say,

> I shall not die, but I shall live,
> and recount the deeds of the Lord. (Ps. 118:17)

You will do this because Jesus has said, "Everyone who lives and believes in me shall never die" (John 11:26).

So what deeds of the Lord will we recount? The deeds of the stone the builders rejected, the one the Lord has made into the cornerstone (Ps. 118:22). We will sing of the saving work of Jesus, not in the earthly temple in Jerusalem but within the gates of the temple the Lord is now building. In the church, among the people of God, we can stand in the presence of God and give thanks to him for the marvelous salvation he has brought and will bring. In the company of God's people, we can speak of Jesus's rejection and exaltation, his death and resurrection, and we can shout,

> This is the day that the Lord has made;
> let us rejoice and be glad in it. (Ps. 118:24)

As we walk through this life, we look forward to the salvation that Jesus will provide. We long for him to return, so we call on him to save us and cause our lives to be lived well in the meanwhile (118:25). We look forward to his coming again in the name of the Lord (118:26) and to the coming festival in God's presence in the heavenly Zion (Ps. 118:27; Heb. 12:22).

We will end where we began. We will give thanks to the Lord, for he is good, for his steadfast love endures forever. At the end of each day, at the end of our lives, in the never ending days of eternity, we will never move beyond or exhaust this truth. We will never stop seeing and feeling that he is good. His goodness will be our joy forever.

Conclusion

This is a psalm of big truths. Jesus saved us. Jesus helps us. Jesus is the cornerstone on which all God's people are built. Jesus has come and will come in the name of the Lord to save and to gather up his people into one. We live surrounded by troubles on every side, but in our Lord we will overcome every one of them.

And through it all, we begin and end in the goodness of God. In our lives and in eternity, in redemption and in glory, in all things we are met with the goodness of God. We live in the goodness of God. We will worship in the goodness of God. There is nothing more to say.

So give thanks to the Lord, for he is good, for his steadfast love endures forever.

Discussion Questions

1. How does Psalm 118 narrate the Christian life?

2. What does it mean for Jesus to be our helper?

3. When will Jesus come in the name of the Lord?

4. What does it mean that God is good?

Conclusion

THE WONDERFUL THING about writing a book like this is that it can surprise you.

When I planned the chapters, I thought I had a good picture of how the author of Hebrews read the Psalms and how the various psalms show Christ. I expected that the author's main interpretive approach would be similar to the Augustinian principle of *totus Christus*—that the psalms refer to the whole of Christ, sometimes in reference to his proper person as the head and sometimes to his body, the church.

While that motif is present, the more closely I looked at the psalms quoted in the letter, the more I got the impression that the author to the Hebrews was reading with the grain of the psalms themselves instead of bringing this one principle to bear in all of them. Because of this, our study of Psalm 40 was not a single story of Christ speaking in the place of his people as I had thought but rather a story of multiple voices, a call and response of the gospel.

The Psalms Together

Another surprise I encountered was that many of the psalms used by Hebrews turned out to be related.

Psalms 2, 45, and 110 are psalms of an exalted king who shares in God's rule, God's name, and God's throne. Psalms 22 and 40 speak of the suffering of a righteous representative and the offering of a sinless body in place of sacrifice. Psalms 8 and 110 end with a human exalted over all creation. Psalms 8 and 95 reflect on the universal human story: from creation to lost glory to promised future redemption to exaltation. Psalms 2, 22, 45, and 102 include the nations coming to praise God—either through the deliverance provided by an individual's death or through the reign of an exalted human king. (Indeed, they come to worship because the king has been delivered through death and raised up!) Psalms 8, 22, 110, and 118 are used by Jesus in the Gospels to describe himself and the things he did. Over the course of this book, Hebrews has taught us, I hope, how to read these psalms. It is worth remembering that, evidently, the author himself learned to read them this way from Jesus.

Psalm 118, the last psalm cited by Hebrews, acts as a review of many of these themes. The psalmist begins praise to God for his enduring love (118:1–4), testifies to God's deliverance as helper and refuge (118:5–9), recounts salvation through hardship even in the face of death and divine discipline (118:10–18), pleads for righteousness and salvation (118:19–25), blesses the one who comes in the name of the Lord (118:26–27), and ends in thanksgiving and praise for God's enduring love (118:28–29).

Through the psalms we have studied, we have seen a man who is both human and God, whose rule determines the fate of nations, who sits at God's right hand as king and priest, who offers his body in the place of all Levitical sacrifices, who occupies the position over creation that humanity was meant to inhabit, who created the world and will make it anew, and who is our help and only offer of eternal rest with God.

The Psalms themselves, taken on their own terms, demand the story of Jesus Christ. No story can explain the Psalms other than the story of the Son of God made man, crucified, risen, and exalted for us and for our salvation.

On Reading the Psalms

In the background of the individual studies of this book, I have been concerned with answering a question: How are we, as Christians, to read the Psalms? Or to put it another way, what does it mean to read the Psalms (or the whole Old Testament) as Christian Scripture?

I hope that reading these psalms with the epistle to the Hebrews has made two things clear: we do not need to bracket Christ out of the Old Testament, nor must we formulate arbitrary rules each time we look for where Jesus might be in a given passage.

It is easy to get the impression that Christological exegesis—the practice of seeing Christ in texts where he is not explicitly mentioned—is arbitrary. To be fair, some often do Christological exegesis arbitrarily. To see Christ in the Old Testament is not the same as reading the Romans Road into every Old Testament passage. It is, rather, to see *Christ*. To see Christ in his fullness, in his two natures, in his person, in his various acts of redemption and rule.

The interpretation of the Psalms in Hebrews has revealed for us several principles for how to rightly see Christ in the Psalms:[1]

1. Look for tensions in the psalm itself. When Psalm 2 speaks of a human king, called Messiah, who determines the fate of nations,

---

[1] This list, derived from this study, will inevitably overlap with other lists about reading the Scriptures Christologically or with older forms of interpretation. See, e.g., the "Classical Christological Toolkit" in R. B. Jamieson's *The Paradox of Sonship: Christology in the Epistle to the Hebrews* (Downers Grove, IL: IVP Academic, 2021), 23–48.

it is proper to ask, "Who is this?" When Psalm 45 presents a human king on his wedding day, who is called God with an eternal throne, it is appropriate to ask, "Who could this be?" When Psalm 22 portrays a human who suffers unto death, is raised up by God, and whose deliverance brings salvation to all the families of the earth, it is right to ask, "About whom . . . does the prophet say this?" (Acts 8:34). Take the texts of the Psalms seriously and demand that they give answers. If, as prophetic texts, the Old Testament does not fully answer these questions, it is right to answer these Old Testament questions with New Testament insights. It is what God intends for us. It is what the whole Scripture is for.

2. Read in light of the whole story of Jesus: the eternal Son of God who assumed humanity, lived, suffered, died, rose again, ascended, and sat at the Father's right hand until his return. Some Old Testament passages will point to the whole story, like Psalm 8. Others will highlight certain aspects, like his death and resurrection in Psalm 22 or his exaltation and session in Psalm 110. All of Jesus's life is for us. All of Jesus's life provides the pattern for the Old Testament.

God as an author delights in repetition of form. The story of Jesus's life is the shape of the story of Israel, which is the shape of the story of humanity, which is the shape of the story of creation. He is the story we cannot help but live.

Whether on the scale of a single chapter or on the scale of cosmic history, the pattern recurs. This is not simply a literary technique that we bring to the Scriptures as interpreters. This is baked into God's world. It is how he made it. If patterning the stories of Scripture on the life of Christ is a literary technique, then most properly it is the technique by which God has written the story of the world.

We too have been made in his image, and the image of God is Christ.[2]

3. Remember the person: something true said of Jesus is always true of Jesus. Something true of Jesus in respect to one of his natures (human or divine) is true of the person. So he who is once called Creator can be seen whenever the Scriptures speak of God creating. Jesus Christ is the same yesterday, today, and forever (Heb. 13:8). So also we can say that the Son of God who has always ruled *became* Son and *became* King, because he did these things as a human.

4. Remember the unity of Jesus and his people. We are his body. Where he is, we are. This is not some wish, projection, or far off hope. In a real sense, we have been raised up and are seated with him in the heavenly places (Eph. 2:6). We are as truly in heaven with Christ now as we are on earth. Even more, what is true of him (in his exalted humanity) will be true of us. When we see him, we will be made like him (1 John 3:2).

Conclusion

The Psalms are made for singing. Yet often, as Christians, we feel strained singing the whole range of the Psalms. What do we do with kings and sacrifices? How do we sing about royal weddings and the judgment of the nations? It can easily feel that the Psalms, or at least many of them, are not meant for us. We retreat to the easy psalms, like 23 and 103, singing or reciting them with zeal while ignoring the great majority of the Psalter that God has provided.

My hope is that this will no longer be the case for you. While I do not pretend to have resolved every difficulty that the Psalms present, I do hope I have given something like a key to open the way.

---

2   Athanasius, *On the Incarnation* 13.20.

CONCLUSION

The Psalms are for us. And they are for us because the Psalter is a book where Jesus is present and is near to us. On every page, he is spoken of, spoken to, or himself speaks. The Psalms are the songs he sings as he leads his people to his Father. They are the hymns he raises for us in the great congregation. They tell of what the Father has told him. And as we sing them, he is the King they herald. He is the righteous sufferer. He is the help of his people. He is the Creator, ruler, judge, and restorer. The Psalms are about him. They are his songs.

We can pick up the Psalter and profit from each and every chapter. We can sing with loud voices and full hearts because when we come to these passages of Scripture, we find that they are truly the songs of the Son.

Appendix

Why Not Psalm 104?

PARTICULARLY ASTUTE READERS, or cross-referencers, will have noticed that there is one psalm cited by Hebrews that we have not studied: Psalm 104. I mentioned it several times (in the chapters on Psalms 45 and 102), but have not considered it at length like the other psalms Hebrews uses. The reason for this is simple. The author's citation of Psalm 104 does not directly say anything about Jesus but rather is used as a foil for the quotations from Psalms 45 and 102.

The author cites Psalm 104:4 in Hebrews 1:7:

Of the angels he says,

> "He makes his angels winds,
> and his ministers a flame of fire."

For the author, this is a comment on the changeability and transience of the angels. God has created them and can make them into whatever he pleases. The angels' changeability is contrasted with the

Son, who has an eternal throne (Heb. 1:8; cf. Ps. 45:6) and who never changes (Heb. 1:10–12; cf. Ps. 102:25–27). I addressed this contrast in both the relevant chapters above.

I chose not to devote a whole chapter to Psalm 104, not because it is undeserving of one, but because of the methodological constraint I set out in the introduction. In this book, I have tried to read the Psalms only in light of the way that Hebrews shows Christ in them. The author to the Hebrews does not comment on how Jesus is present in Psalm 104 but only on what God (likely the Father) says about the angels. Since Hebrews 1:7 does not shed light on Jesus's activity in Psalm 104, I left it out of this book.

That is not to say that Jesus is absent from Psalm 104. Psalm 104 is about God's creation and goodness to all he has made. In both Psalms 102 and 104, creation is described as setting foundations (Ps. 102:25; 104:5). We know that God created the world and laid its foundation through Jesus (Heb. 1:2, 10). Furthermore, Psalm 104:24 speaks of how the Lord made all his works "in wisdom." Historically, this has been interpreted as God's creation of the world through Christ who is the wisdom of God (Col. 2:3), which is another way of saying that God created the world through his Word (John 1:1–3).

Psalm 104 certainly can, and should, be read as another song of Jesus. It is only for reasons of method that it did not receive a full study in this book. But there is nothing stopping you from diving into it. It may be a wonderful next step.

Further Reading

THE HISTORY OF THE CHURCH is filled with Christ-exalting readings of the Psalms. The following books are works that I have found particularly helpful and encouraging. While there are doubtless many books I could have recommended in this section, these three have most shaped my own thought on the Psalms over the course of preparing for this book. You will note that none of them are recent. This is not because nothing good has been written on the Psalms recently—far to the contrary—but rather because I wanted my reading of the Psalms to be shaped by the way the church has read the Psalms across place and time.

Augustine. *Expositions of the Psalms.* 6 vols. Translated by Maria Boulding. Edited by John E. Rotelle. New York: New City Press, 2000–2004.

Augustine's commentary stands at the head of so much of the western Christian tradition's reading of the Psalter. I have found him valuable in two ways: his insight and his strangeness. What I mean is that Augustine always reads the Psalms with one eye on Christ and another on his congregation. Because of this, he sometimes sees Christ in the Psalms in places where I would not (and even in places where I doubt he is in fact there), and he sometimes sees too much of his own day's controversies. Even in the midst of this, however, his genuine spiritual insight, immense familiarity with the breadth of Scripture, and theological genius come through in encouraging, entertaining, and fascinating sermons on the Psalms.

Calvin, John. *Commentary on the Book of Psalms*. 5 vols. Translated by James Anderson. Grand Rapids, MI: Eerdmans, 1949.
Calvin's commentary, as with much of his work, is theologically precise, linguistically informed, and pastorally aimed. Standing at the head of the Reformed tradition, Calvin deftly reads the Psalms theologically while still being grounded in the original composition of the Psalms as God's songs for his old covenant people.

Spurgeon, Charles Haddon. *The Treasury of David*. Peabody, MA: Hendrickson Academic, 1990.
Spurgeon's *Treasury* surprised me. This prince of modern preachers was as committed to reading the Psalms as Jesus's book as was Augustine more than a millennium before him. He saw the Psalms as full of the beauty of Jesus and so proclaimed them as beautiful. This set of expositions shows one way that, in times close to ours, the Psalms can and have been preached in a way that is theologically sensitive, Christologically rich, and filled with the whole story of Scripture.

General Index

Aaronic priesthood, 119, 134
Abraham, 48, 117–18
Adam, 30–31
adversaries, 132
Ahab, 115
allusions, 7, 121
angels, 16, 28, 29–30, 31, 72, 73, 106, 115, 122–23, 153–54
Anglican church, 80
Anointed One, 11, 12, 13–14, 15, 70
anxiety, 99–100
apostles, 1–2, 5
atonement, 56
Augustine, 128n3, 147, 155–56
authority, 114–15

Babel, 13, 102
Babylon, 13
beauty, 35, 68, 71–72
Bible
   and family devotions, 79
   patterns in, 51, 115
   rereading of, 6
   story of, 23
big words, 131–32
blessedness, 16
breathtaking, 65–66
bride, 71, 75

Caleb, 86
Calvin, John, 69, 156
celebration, 139
chiasm, 99n1
Christian life, 133, 143

Christian worship, 3
Christie, Agatha, 6
Christological readings, 149
Christology, 12
christos, 11
church
   as body of Christ, 147
   as bride of Christ, 75–76
   and presence of God, 145
citation, 72, 108, 121, 122, 140, 141, 153
clichés, 65
clusters, 52
conquest, 15
contentment, 140
contrasting speech, 10
control, 21–22, 29, 32
conversion, 128
covenant mediator, 45
creation, 27–28, 83, 90, 154
curse, 87, 92

darkness, 132
David, 4, 8, 11–12, 13, 17, 22–28, 41, 45, 47, 49, 53, 61–62, 90, 112, 113, 114
Davidic covenant, 14, 114
Day of Atonement, 59
death, 31, 42, 104, 111
deliverance, 43, 44, 52, 53, 54–55, 57, 61, 91, 102, 103, 104
depression, 99–100
disobedience, 89, 92
distress, 98, 136
divine name, 113–14
dominion, 27, 31

GENERAL INDEX

echoes, 7
enemies, 24–25, 37, 115–17, 127, 128, 144
Enoch, 51
enthronement, 107, 122–24, 125
eschatology, 126
evil, 13
exaltation, 18, 26, 32, 74, 144–45
exegesis, 8, 149
exile, 101

faith, 41
family devotions, 79
feasts, 139
first reading, 6, 112
framing, 112

gender, 76–77
genealogies, 51
genre, 51–52
Gentile mission, 48
God
  absence of, 38–39, 45, 46
  eternal stability of, 105, 106, 108, 109
  glory of, 22, 24, 101, 103
  goodness of, 39, 54, 58, 61, 62, 128, 132–34, 139, 141, 143, 146
  as king, 82
  love of, 23, 26, 134
  majesty of, 24
  power of, 83, 84, 109
  presence of, 90, 91, 93, 97, 103, 137, 145
  promises of, 117
  right hand of, 114–15, 124, 129
  voice of, 8
  wrath of, 36, 89
gospel, 63, 107–8, 109, 127, 147
grass, 99, 104, 110
gratitude, 56
Greek language, 91
Greek Psalms, 60–61
Gregory of Nazianzus, 30

hardship, 132
heavens, 25, 27
Hebrew language, 60–61
Hebrews, 2, 16–18, 28–30, 59–61, 72–75, 87–91, 105–8, 121–25, 139–43
helper, 136, 141, 143, 144
holiness, 119

human heart, 11
humanity
  dominion of, 27, 28, 29
  exaltation of, 32
  history of, 31
  weakness of, 23, 24
hymns, 152

image of God, 28, 31, 32, 77, 84, 151
impermanence, 99
incarnation, 18, 19, 30–31, 60, 74
insecurity, 140
intra-psalter, 107
isolation, 100

Jesus Christ
  crucifixion of, 36–37, 41, 49
  death and resurrection of, 5, 28, 45, 46–47, 49, 63, 145
  divinity of, 73–74, 108, 151
  eternal sonship of, 17–18
  following of, 140
  as helper, 143
  incarnation of, 18, 19, 30–31, 60, 74
  as king, 75, 126
  as priest, 141
  in the Psalms, 3
  second coming of, 143
  session of, 124–25
  story of, 149, 150
  superiority of, 5, 7, 16–17, 28, 106, 122–23
Joshua, 86, 91, 92
joy, 139, 146
Judaism, 36
judgment, 10, 14–15, 20, 80, 92, 120–21, 127–28

kingdom of God, 116
kings, 9, 13, 45, 69, 70, 72

Levi, 124
Levitical sacrifices, 59, 60, 61, 148
love song, 66, 67–68

Macbeth, 131–32
Massah, 85
Melchizedek, 117, 118–19, 124
men, 76–77
Meribah, 85

GENERAL INDEX

Messiah, 11, 129, 149
Micaiah, 115
money, 140
moon, 25, 27, 35, 37
morning prayers, 79–80
Moses, 45, 81, 86
mystery, 111, 112, 119

narrative, 1
nations, 9, 10, 11, 18, 47–48, 105, 148
new covenant, 75
New Testament, 1–5, 9, 17, 19, 24, 48, 112, 124, 142, 150

oaths, 117
obedience, 56
offering, 56, 63
Old Testament
    as Christian Scripture, 2
    New Testament's use of, 1
    offerings of, 56
    as pointing to Christ, 2, 59, 126, 149–50
opening line, 36

pain, 22, 98
paradox, 23
patterns, 51, 115, 150
people of God, 75, 151
persecution, 18–19, 99
poetry, 1, 55, 65, 66
posterity, 76, 77
praise, 66, 81, 82
priests, 119, 124–25
prince, 72
prophecy, 36, 37, 45, 49, 121
prophets, 2, 45, 47, 60, 70, 75, 114
propitiation, 56
protection, 140
Psalms
    as hymnbook of Christ, 2, 3–4, 152
    opening line of, 36
    reading as Christian Scripture, 149–51
psalms of Asaph, 52

quotation, 4, 7, 18, 60, 153

rebellion, 10, 13, 18, 19
reconciliation, 15
redemption, 15, 19, 36, 81, 92
repentance, 10, 16, 52, 100

repetition, 132, 136, 150
rest, 80, 87, 89, 93
restoration, 37
resurrection, 18, 46–47, 74, 77, 145
revelation, 19, 74
reversal, 42
righteousness, 9, 62, 69
right hand, 114
Roman Catholics, 79–80

Sabbath rest, 90–91
sacrifice, 55–57, 62, 124, 138–39
salvation, 10, 14, 19, 38, 41, 43, 46, 57, 109, 138
scepters, 9, 116, 127
second reading, 5–6
Shakespeare, William, 131
shame, 39
shepherds, 84
sin
    anger against, 108
    awareness of, 63
    curse of, 31
    as futile, 13
    purification for, 122, 123
    and suffering, 99
singing, 152
smallness, 95–96, 101
Solomon, 17, 69
songs of ascents, 52
son of man, 29
sonship, 16, 18, 120
Sons of Korah, 68
space, 25, 82
Spurgeon, C. H., 52–53, 156
stars, 22, 25, 27, 65, 105
steadfast love, 134, 139, 145–46
subjection, 29
suffering, 19, 38, 39, 46, 96, 97, 98, 99, 100, 103, 110, 132, 144

temple, 145
tensions, 149–50
thanksgiving, 51, 53, 54, 56
themes, 6, 148
Theophylact, 4
thrones, 9, 107, 122–24, 125
totus Christus, 147
Trinity, 4, 74, 114
trust, 40, 140

typology, 45, 47, 69

unbelief, 89, 92
universe, 25–26
Uriah, 13

victory, 121, 127
vindication, 37, 44
violence, 42

wealth, 140
wedding, 65–66, 71, 76, 77
wickedness, 9, 10, 13, 14, 15, 20
wilderness generation, 86–87, 89, 90
wisdom, 154
women, 76–77
world, 10
worship, 3, 43, 44, 47, 81, 82, 93, 103, 109, 136, 137

Scripture Index

Genesis
1 90
1:26–27 27
1:28 27
2:3 90
5 51
6:2 16
6:4 16
11:1–9 13
11:5 102
11:7 102
14 118
14:17–20 118
14:18 118
14:19 118
14:22 118
22 117
22:15–19 118

Exodus
17 85
17:1–7 85
17:2 86
17:3 86
17:7 86

Numbers
14:26–38 86

Deuteronomy
32:8 16

1 Samuel
15:22 56

2 Samuel
7 118
7:4–17 118
7:13 14
7:14 . . . . 14, 18

1 Kings
15:4–5 41
22:19 115

Job
1:6 . . . . 16, 115
2:1 16
38:7 16

Psalms
1 9
2 . . . . 9, 19, 48, 52, 112, 120, 121, 148
2:1 11
2:1–3 10–11
2:2 11
2:4–6 10
2:4–9 12
2:5 13
2:6 13
2:7 . . . . 10, 14, 16, 17
2:7–9 . . . . 10, 17, 19
2:8 14
2:8–9 14
2:9 . . . . 14, 121
2:10–12 . . . . . . 10, 15
7:8 62
8 . . . . 22, 29, 31, 52, 148
8:1 32
8:1–4 23
8:2 24
8:3 . . . . 25, 27
8:4 25
8:5 . . . . 27, 30
8:5–9 . . . . 23, 26
8:6 27
8:7–8 27
8:9 . . . . 27, 32
18:20 62
18:24 62
18:50 11
20:6 11
22 . . . . 35, 36, 37, 41, 43, 44–45, 48, 49, 52, 54, 57, 107, 148, 150
22:1 . . . . 36, 46, 47
22:1–21 38
22:3–11 38–39
22:8 . . . . 39, 41
22:12–18 40
22:13 42
22:14 41

22:15 41	45:10 71	103 151
22:17 41	45:10–17 70–71	104 . . . . 153, 154
22:18 41	45:12 71	104:4 153
22:19–21 41–42	45:15 72	104:5 154
22:21 42	45:16 71	110 . . . . 112, 113,
22:22 . . . . 43, 46	51 63	115, 120,
22:25 47	70 53	121, 122,
22:25–31 43–44	73–83 52	125, 126,
22:27 . . . . 44, 47, 107	82:6 69	127, 128,
22:28 107	89:20 11	129, 148
22:30 48	95 . . . . 79, 82, 87,	110:1 . . . . 113, 116,
22:31 . . . . 44, 47, 48	89, 90, 91,	123, 124, 125
23 . . . . 112, 151	92, 148	110:2 . . . . 116, 126
26:11 62	95:1 83	110:2–4 115–16
38 63	95:1–7 81	110:3 . . . . 116, 119–20
39 53	95:3 . . . . 82, 83	110:4 . . . . 116, 117,
39:12 53	95:4 82	118, 121,
40 . . . . 52, 53, 54,	95:5 83	124, 125
55, 60, 61,	95:6 84	110:5 121
63, 147, 148	95:7 84	110:5–6 . . . . 127, 128n3
40:1 53	95:7–8 85	110:5–7 120
40:1–5 . . . . 53–54, 63	95:7–11 85	110:6 121
40:2 54	95:11 . . . . 80, 87, 90	118 . . . . 132, 142,
40:3 54	102 . . . . 72, 96, 103,	143, 148
40:4–5 . . . . 54, 55	106, 107,	118:1–4 . . . . 133, 148
40:5 54	108, 109,	118:5–7 144
40:6 . . . . 52, 56, 57,	153, 154	118:5–9 148
60	102:1–2 96–97	118:5–18 134–35
40:6–8 61	102:3–17 97–98	118:6 136
40:6–10 . . . . 53, 55, 63	102:4 99	118:6–7 140
40:8 57	102:6 100	118:7 136
40:9–10 57	102:7 . . . . 99n1, 100	118:8 136
40:11 63	102:8 100	118:9 136
40:11–17 . . . . . . 53, 57–58,	102:9 99	118:10 . . . . 136, 144
63	102:11 99	118:10–12 144
40:12 59	102:12 . . . . 100, 106n2	118:10–18 148
42–43 52	102:13 101	118:11 . . . . 136, 144
45 . . . . 66, 69, 72,	102:14 101	118:12 . . . . 136, 144
75, 77, 106,	102:16 101	118:15 136
107, 148,	102:17 101	118:15–16 144
150, 153	102:18–22 101–2	118:16 . . . . 136, 144
45:1–5 67	102:19 102	118:17 145
45:2 70	102:20 103	118:19–25 148
45:4 68	102:21 103	118:19–27 136–37
45:6 . . . . 69, 70, 154	102:22 103	118:21 137
45:6–9 68–69	102:23–28 103–4	118:22 145
45:7 . . . . 69, 70	102:25 154	118:22–23 142
45:8–9 69	102:28 105	118:22–24 138

118:24 . . . . 138, 145
118:25 145
118:26 . . . . 138, 142, 145
118:26–27 148
118:27 . . . . 138, 145
118:28–29 . . . . . 139, 148
120–134 52

Isaiah
6:1 115
13:1–22 13
53 44
34:11 100
62:5 75

Ezekiel
1:26 115
23 75

Hosea
2–4 75

Amos
3:12 42

Zephaniah
2:14 100

Matthew
1 51
5:11–12 18
12:42 17
18:1–10 24
21:16 24
21:42 142
22:45 113
23:37–39 142
27:35 41
27:41–44 41
27:46 36
27:60 41

Mark
4:17 18
12:10–11 142
15:24 41
15:46 41

Luke
11:31 17
11:49 19
15:20 103
20:17 142
22:17–20 118
23:34 41
23:53 41

John
1:1 . . . . 6, 19
1:1–3 154
2:19–22 . . . . 14n1
6:53–58 119
11:26 145
12:49 19
14:7–9 19
15:20 19
19:24 41
19:41–42 41

Acts
1:8 127
2:30 47
8:34 . . . . 44, 150

Romans
3:21–22 . . . . 48n2
4:25 . . . . 48n2
8:19–23 27

1 Corinthians
3:16–17 . . . . 14n1

Galatians
2:20 128

Ephesians
2:6 151
2:11–22 48
2:13–22 . . . . 14n1
5:25–32 75

Colossians
1:13 127
1:17 83
2:3 154

2 Timothy
2:12 76
3:12 19

Hebrews
1 72
1:1–4 122
1:2 . . . . 122, 154
1:3 . . . . 19, 74, 122
1:3–4 122
1:5 . . . . 16, 18, 73
1:7 . . . . 153, 154
1:7–8 105–6
1:7–9 73
1:8 . . . . 73, 154
1:9 73
1:10 154
1:10–12 106
1:13 123
2 30
2:5–8 28
2:8 29
2:9 . . . . 30, 31
2:10 32
2:10–12 . . . . 46, 48
2:11 49
2:11–12 47
2:14–18 30
2:18 141
3:7–4:11 89
3:12–4:11 87–88
4 89
4:1 89
4:8 91
4:16 141
5:6 124
5:7 47
5:10 124
6:20 . . . . 32, 124
7:11 124
7:16 124
7:17 124
7:21 124
8:1 123
9:6–14 124
9:12 124
10 59

SCRIPTURE INDEX

10:1–10 124
10:3–10 59–60
10:5 60
10:11–14 125
10:12–13 123
12:2 . . . . 32, 123

12:22 145
12:22–23 48
13 140
13:5–6 139
13:8 . . . . 108, 141, 151

1 John
3:2 151

Revelation
20:6 76
21:9–22:17 75